SENSA

The Language of the Sacred Mysteries

Dorje Jinpa

Pentarba Publications

Also by Dorje Jinpa

SENSA: The Language of the Sacred Mysteries

A Synthesis of Alchemy: An Inquiry into the Secrets of Hermetic Philosophy

Essential Teachings of Maitreya: Three Complete Works

Secrets of the Heart: Awakening to Enlightenment

The Book of Hermes

The Coming Avatar: An Essay on the Reappearance of the Christ

Knights of the Sacred Fire: An Introduction to the Agni Yoga Teachings

Gates to Infinity: A Commentary on the Agni Yoga Infinity Teachings

Available at pentarba.com

"SENSA is a jewel of a book."   —The Beacon: A Magazine of Esoteric Philosophy.

"One of the most important books I have read in recent years."   —Martin Viewg, co-author of *When the Soul Awakens*.

"The SENSA book is amazing."   —Lars Muhi, author of *The Law of Light*.

"Profound…"   —*Steiner Books*

"Impressive."   —Gesine Abrahm, author of *Keeping the Magic Alive*.

"Your SENSA book was brilliant."   —Donna Mitchell-Moniak author of *Astrology Illuminated*.

"Answers lingering esoteric questions with the greatest clarity."   —Nancy Seifer co-author of *When the Soul Awakens*.

"SENSA is a must-read for all serious esoteric students…"
     —John Nash for *The Esoteric Quarterly*

© Pentarba Publications

Sold online at pentarba.com

pentarbapublications@gmail.com

300 copies, hardback 2012

Second Revised Edition, 100 copies, paperback 2019

50 copies, paperback 2020

100 copies, hardback 2003

Cover painting Comte de St. Germain from his
The Devine Threefold Sophia

The true science of words and sounds has been lost, but not irretrievably so. In the ages to come it will be recovered once again, creating thereby a greater union and harmony between heaven and earth, between the angels and humanity, and between all the nations and peoples of the world. The Holy Tongue, lost and forgotten, will be spoken again in all its purity, and the prophecies found in the sacred scriptures will be fulfilled.

Sepher ha Zohar (The Book of Light)

Contents

The Law of Correspondence 7

The Language of the Gods 38

The Creative WORD 78

Mind and the Geometry of Sound. 125

Sensa Script. 154

Archetypal Signatures of Living Organisms. 190

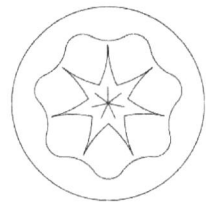

The Law of Correspondence

That which is above is like that which is below and that which is below is like that which is above. In this is expressed the miracle of the one.   Hermes Trismegistus

When the Elohim created the world they made the lower world as a reflection of the higher. Thus they established a direct correspondence between the higher and the lower worlds as between the higher and lower letters of the spiritual language with which they created the world.

Sepher ha Zohar (The Book of Light)

A symbol is an outer visible sign of an inner spiritual reality.   Brother
D.K.

All esoteric teachings are based upon the correspondence that exists between the macrocosm and the microcosm.

Rudolf Steiner

In the same way that an acorn contains the complete archetypal impulses for the evolution of an oak tree, so does the seed of the human spirit contain the blueprints for the spiritual evolution of humanity. All living organisms, without exception, follow the pattern of growth predetermined by their seeds. To understand the nature and purpose of Evolution, therefore, we must first examine its seeds. In the ancient Mystery Schools an understanding of the primary keynotes of nature, its seeds, was greatly facilitated through the use of symbols. In the same way that science relies upon the language of mathematics to give a precise and accurate description of its findings, so the scientists of the ancient Wisdom Religion, in order to accurately express their understanding of fundamental laws and principles, made use of the natural language inherent in the geometric structure of Nature Herself. These symbolic formulas were based upon the axiom expressed by Plato that 'God Geometrizes;' meaning that everything in Nature follows the basic geometric patterns set for it upon the archetypal planes of existence. This natural language, which has always been kept secret from the uninitiated, differs fundamentally from other languages in that its symbols do not arbitrarily represent objects, *but rather the original archetypal patterns from which the objects are formed.*

The languages of the world have evolved almost entirely in response to the material world and are therefore rarely applicable to the higher dimensions of non-physical reality. Whenever mystic seers attempt to describe their vision of the higher worlds, for example, they must do so, for the most part, symbolically, in the language of analogy, using symbols to represent higher corresponding truths. Manly P. Hall, in his monumental work on the Mysteries, *The Secret Teachings of All Ages,* writes.

> Symbolism is the language of the Mysteries; in fact it is the language not only of mysticism and philosophy but of all Nature, for every law and power active in universal procedure is manifested to the limited sense perceptions of man through the medium of symbols. Every form existing in the diversified sphere of being is symbolic of the divine activity by which it is produced. By symbols men have ever sought to communicate to each other those thoughts that transcend the limitations of language. Rejecting man-conceived dialects as inadequate and

unworthy to perpetuate divine ideas, the Mysteries thus chose symbols as a far more ingenious and ideal method of preserving their transcendental knowledge. In a single figure a symbol may both reveal and conceal, for to the wise the subject of a symbol is obvious, while to the ignorant the figure remains inscrutable.

Kenneth Mackenzie in his book *The Royal Masonic Cyclopedia*, first published in 1877, states:

> All esoteric societies have made use of emblems and symbols, such as the Pythagorean Society, the Eleusinian, the Hermetic Brethren of Egypt, the Rosicrucians and the Freemasons. Many of these emblems it is not proper to divulge to the general eye, and a very minute difference may make the emblem or symbol differ widely in its meaning. The magical sigilla, being founded on certain principles of numbers, partake of this character, and although monstrous or ridiculous in the eyes of the uninstructed, convey a whole body of doctrine to those who have been trained to recognize them.

To understand the true nature of symbols as the outer visible signs of inner realities we must first discover the key to their essential nature. "The key that is to open one," says Homer, "must open all. Otherwise it is not the right key." The master key to understanding the true nature of symbols, as well as the principles they represent, is the law of correspondence. This law demonstrates the fundamental truth that everything in the physical world (the microcosm) is a direct proportioned reflection of a higher correspondence in the spiritual world (the macrocosm).

Alfred Schmid in his *The Marvel of Light*, a beautiful work on the synthesis of physics and metaphysics, states:

For the Gnostic it is of significance that the visible world is analogous to the invisible, or, more simply stated: the universe is made in the image of the cosmic order.[1]

According to Iamblichus, a fourth century Egyptian Initiate, Pythagoras taught the principle of correspondence in his secret school. The Sufis, an esoteric linage that can be traced back to the Magi of ancient Persia, also taught this principle. Abu Bakr Siraj Ed-Din in his Sufi classic, *The Book of Certainty*, which is based to a large extent upon the esoteric writings of one the greatest of all Sufi masters, Muhyiddin Ibn 'Arabi (1165-1240), illustrates this truth:

> Symbols have the power to remind [us] of their counterparts in the higher worlds, not through mere incidental resemblance but because they are actually related to them in the way that a shadow is related to the object which casts it. There is not the least thing in existence that is not such a shadow.... Nor is there anything that is any more than a shadow. Indeed, if a world did not cast down shadows from above, the worlds below it would at once vanish altogether, since each world in creation is no more than an issue of shadows entirely dependent on the archetypes in the world above.[2]

Ibn 'Arabi says that when the term *'mathal,'* which means 'symbolic likeness,' is used in the Quran it refers to "the essential or vertical likeness that exists between the higher and lower worlds." In other words a symbolic image (*mathal*) manifests according to the law of analogy or correspondence (*'alm al-mathal*). In the Quran it was often used along with a word or symbolic phrase to refer the reader to that symbol's higher or lower corresponding meaning.[3]

---

[1] East-West Publications, 1984.
[2] Rider London, 1952 Page 50
[3] See The Quram 2:24-26, 13:3, & 47:15

The terms 'occult' and 'esoteric' refer to the subtle truths hidden behind symbols. One of the advantages of esoteric writing, besides veiling truths that are inappropriate for general use, is that a lot of essential information can be stated briefly and simply. A well-presented symbol can represent to the intuitive awareness a vast hierarchy of corresponding levels of meaning. Abu Bakr Siraj Ed-Din continues:

> It is by reason of the correspondence between the two worlds that sacred utterances, which refer directly to the macrocosm, may be interpreted as referring also to the microcosm. For example one may say that the Fountain of Immortality which springs from the centre of the Garden of Eden is the counterpart of the Eye of Certainty in the centre of the true man's soul, or rather that this Eye is itself the real Fountain of Immortality, of which the Fountain of Eden is an outward reflection, and so when it is said that Adam was driven out of the Garden of Eden, the meaning is that man in general had lost the inward paradise of the Eye as well as the Paradise of the outer world.[1]

Proclus (412-485 AD) the illuminated interpreter of the teachings of Plato and the Pythagoreans, in the opening lines of his book, *A Dissertation on Theurgy*, states:

> In the same way that lovers of beauty gradually advance from the beauty which is apparent to the senses to that beauty which is divine; so the ancient priests, gradually advanced from an understanding that there exists a certain correspondence and sympathy between natural things and things occult, to the discovery that all is contained in all. *From this mutual sympathy and correspondence they fabricated their sacred sciences.* Thus they recognized things supreme in such as are subordinate and the subordinate in the supreme.

---

[1] *The Book of Certainty*, Abu Bakr Siraj Ed-Din. P. 32-33.

St. Augustine, who was greatly influenced by the writings of Plato and the Neo-Platonic philosophers, states in his *De Musica* that the function of geometry in art, architecture, and music lies in its analogical relationship with spiritual principles, which has the ability to lead the mind from the world of appearances to the contemplation of the divine order behind it. *True beauty*, he said, *is anchored in spiritual reality*. When the created physical form, whether in painting, architecture, or music, corresponds to divine principles, beauty is the result. This idea became the central theme and motivating impulse behind the high Renaissance of Europe. The structural designs of the great gothic cathedrals were successfully based upon this principle. Leonardo Da Vinci, Raphael, Durer, and many other great artists of that period affirmed it as the basis of their aesthetics and art. They sought to create audible and visual echoes of metaphysical perfection by following what the Pythagorean mystics ascribed to the sacred science of polarity, number, and harmonic proportion. They applied the same correspondences that naturally exist between celestial and audible harmonics to their art and architecture. Just as religious icons were thought to partake of a portion of the sacred reality they represented, so the visual and audible proportions of divine harmonics when applied to their art were thought to partake of the metaphysical truths with which they corresponded.

Otto von Simon, in his illuminating book *The Gothic Cathedral: Origins of Gothic Architecture and Medieval Concepts of Order,* gives some hints as to the worldview and motivating impulse behind the designs of some of the great cathedrals of Europe. The idea, says Simon, was to create a true "symbol of the kingdom of God on earth." These temple builders felt that because everything natural was a reflection of the spiritual world, then the house of God should correspond as close as possible to the archetypal forms of the spiritual world. One of the ways this could be done, they reasoned, was by translating the natural harmonies of musical consonance into geometric and architectural relationships. This idea they called 'commodulatio' or 'symmetria.'

The Rosicrucians also taught this principle. Thomas Vaughn, in his *Coelum Terrae* or *Heaven to Earth* quotes from a letter that he received from his Rosicrucian teacher, who he called 'The Kabalist:'

The building of the sanctuary, which is here below is framed according to that of the Sanctuary, which is above.

Thomas Vaughn clarifies this by stating:

> Here we have two worlds, two universal Natures, visible and invisible, out of which both of those worlds proceeded. The passive universal nature was made in the image of the active universal one and the conformity of both worlds or 'sanctuaries' consists in the original conformity of their principles. [1]

In the secret Mystery schools the principles of archetypal symbolism were used to understand and apply the correspondences that naturally exists between planes, dimensions, and levels of being. Plato, who by his own semi-veiled account had been initiated into the Mysteries in Egypt, said that the analogical agreement that exists between a divine paradigm and its reflection in form is called 'geometrical equality,' which he said was 'mighty among both the Gods and men.'

The material world, says Plato in his Dialogue on Nature (*Timeous*), is an image, a reflection, of a portion of the mental world. This, he says, take place by the intellectual gods pouring forth a likeness of the divine paradigm into form upon the physical plane via the elemental gods. The term 'paradigm,' as used in Greek metaphysics, refers to the innate archetypal thought-forms, the blueprints from which the manifestation of the phenomenal universe arises. It does not mean 'a working theory of reality' as the term is so often misused today. Paradigms are reflected images of the impulses behind evolution. Plato called them idea-forms (*eidos*). Iamblichus, the author of *The Life of Pythagoras* and *The Egyptian Mysteries*, writes:

> The construction and composition of the universe and everything in it was wrought by the creative mind in the likeness and number of the perfect and divine paradigm.[2]

---

[1] *The Works of Thomas Vaughan*, University Books, 1968, page 192.
[2] *The Theology of Arithmetic.*

One of the more obvious examples of the law of correspondence can be seen between an atom of matter and a solar system. And although this analogy exists between two aspects of the physical universe it nevertheless demonstrates to some degree the principles involved. Sir James Jeans, the distinguished British scientist, explains:

> In the universe around us the attraction between electric charges of opposite signs, positive and negative, follows, as it happens, precisely the same law as gravitation, the attraction falling off as the inverse square of the distance between two charges. Thus the nucleus-electron system [of an atom] is similar in all respects to a sun-planet system.

Another obvious example of this law can be observed is the way notes of the seven toned musical scale correspond in kind to their higher and lower octaves. Pythagoras is said to have used the example of octaves and harmonic ratios to teach celestial harmonics and the analogical structure of the cosmos. Pythagoras, through his understanding of the Law of Analogy, could apply the laws of musical harmonies to an understanding of the nature of the Music of the Spheres. Robert Fludd, who was a student of Rosicrucian philosophy, in the *Temple of Music* demonstrates his understanding of the correspondences that exist between celestial and audible harmonics:

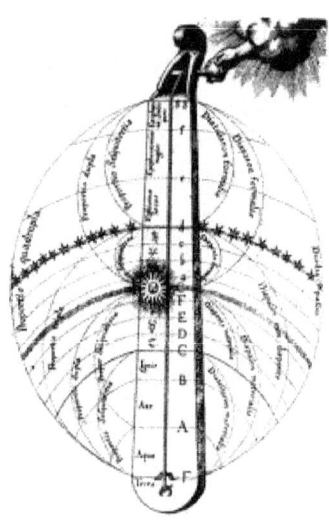

Manly P. Hall, in his chapter on *The Pythagorean Theory of Music and Color*, points to an area of harmonic correspondence that has been verified by mainstream science:

> A notable example of modern corroboration of ancient philosophical teaching is that of the progression of the elements according to harmonic ratios. While making a list of the elements in the ascending order of their atomic weights, John A. Newlands discovered at every eighth element a distinct repetition of properties. This discovery is known as the *law of octaves* in modern chemistry.[1]

Brother Djwhal Khul affirms the importance of the Law of Analogy in his monumental work, *Treatise on Cosmic Fire,* published in 1925 under the name of his student, Alice Bailey:

> A study of the laws of correspondence and analogy is the one thread by which we can find our way through the labyrinth and the one ray of light that shines through the darkness of the

[1] *The Secret Teachings of All Ages.* Philosophical Research Society, 1928, Page LXXXII.

surrounding ignorance.... In the study of this law we need to remember that the correspondence lies in its essence and not in the exoteric working out of details.[1]

The Law of Correspondence is infallible if rightly approached and applied.[2]

H. P. Blavatsky, the initiate founder of Theosophy, an organization based upon brotherhood and the essential unity of all religions, says that the Law of Analogy is "the first and most important key to cosmic physics." In a talk before the Esoteric Section of the Theosophical Society she states:

> One who comprehends well the above explanations will readily see how important it is for every student, whether he is striving for practical occult powers or only for the purely psychic and spiritual gifts of clairvoyance and metaphysical knowledge, to master thoroughly the right correspondence between the human or natural principles and those of Cosmos.[3]

Initiates of the Mysteries are taught that the true laws of nature are not physical at all, that the physical plane is merely a plane of effects produced by causes originating from higher planes of consciousness and being and that even the laws of evolution as perceived by material scientists are but reflections of higher laws of spiritual evolution. The Sufis rightly maintain that the science of correspondence (*alm al-Mathal*) is based upon the greater science of universal equilibrium (*'ilm al-mizan*), which governs the inner and outer harmony of the cosmos. Henry Corbin, a gifted esoteric interpreter of the Sufi doctrine, devotes a chapter to this idea in his book, *Temple and Contemplation*.[4]

---

[1] (See pages 245-359).

[2] Rays and Initiations. Page 180.

[3] *Collected Writings* Volume XII, page 566. Theosophical Publishing House 1980

[4] *The Science of Balance and Correspondences between Worlds in Islamic Gnosis*, pages 55-131

In Islamic gnosis...the balance of the things religious *(mizan al-diyanah)* makes it possible to specify the correspondence between the earthly esoteric hierarchy and the celestial angelic hierarchy and more generally the correspondences between the spiritual and corporal worlds. The visual aspect of a being presupposes its equilibration by an invisible and celestial counterpart; the apparent and exoteric *(zahir)* is balanced by the occulted and esoteric *(batin)*.
1

Albert Pike, who has written extensively on the Sacred Mysteries from the perspective of Masonry, writes:

The Royal Secret...is as the Sohar[2] terms the Mystery of Balance. It is the secret of Universal Equilibrium.[3]

The law of correspondence is one of the central themes of Hermetic Science. Hermes Trismegistus, the Grand Hierophant of the Egyptian Mysteries, affirms this law in the opening lines of his famous *Emerald Tablet*:

That which is above is like that which is below,
And that which is below is like that which is above,
Thus is produced the miracle of the one thing.

The *Kalachakra Tantra*, an esoteric scripture traditionally attributed to the Buddha, expresses this truth by stating: "As it is in the outer world so it is with the inner world of man."[4] The Hindu scripture *Shaiva Siddhanta* states the principle in this way: "What is in man corresponds to what is in the universe."[5] An advanced yoga technique

---

[1] Page 57.

[2] *Book of Light (Sepher ha Zohar)*

[3] *Morals and Dogma of the Ancient and Accepted Scottish rite of Freemasonry.* Pages 858-859.

[4] Quoted by Glenn H. Mullin in his *The Practice of Kalachakra*, page 154

[5] *Pathanjali Sarkam, Koil Puranam, 70*

of Kashmir Shaivism called *Karana* instructs the yogi to contemplate the body, along with its nerve centers, as a replica of the cosmos.[1]

Akshaya Banerjea, in his brilliant chronicle on the writings of Gorakhnath, one of the greatest of Hindu yogis, writes:

> Goraknath and the Siddha Yogi school conceive the individual human body as an epitome of the cosmic body of Shiva-Shakti. A Yogi can, through the intensive practice of contemplation and meditation, realize the whole universe within himself and identify himself with the whole universe. All worlds in the cosmic system, all orders of existences, all planes of experiences, are in some mysterious way represented within the fully developed human body. Though apparently occupying a small portion of space, though living for a short period of time on the gross earthly plane, the human body is a fine mirror of the *maha-sakara-pinda* of Shiva-Shakti.[2]

Simply stated the law of correspondence asserts that the microcosm or lesser material universe is formed in a direct corresponding likeness to the macrocosm, the greater spiritual world. The same laws, the same fundamental energy patterns and geometrical theorems apply to both of these worlds, as well as to each plane of existence—not in detail but in their essential natures.

In esoteric Buddhism the realization of this truth is called 'Mirror-like Wisdom' (*Adarsa-jnana*), one of the five levels of understanding taught by the Buddha. Its symbol is the crescent moon. In the same way that the moon has no light of its own but merely reflects the light of the sun, so the material and conceptual world having no life of its own merely reflects the life of the spiritual world, the *Dharmadhatu*, symbolized by the sun. In the Buddhist scriptures 'Mirror-like wisdom' is said to be the realization of the essential unity

---

[1] See page 37 of Abhinavagupts's *Paratrisika Vivarana,* translated with extensive notes by Jaideva Singh, Motilal Bararsidass 2005

[2] *Philosophy of Gorakhnath with Goraksha-Vacana-Sangraha.* Mahant Dig Vijai Nath Trust.

of the 'two truths,' the ultimate truth (which does not change) and relative truth (which is in constant change). This unified relationship is symbolically represented as a sun disk over a crescent moon: . According to the *Kalachakra Tantra* the vibrational frequency of this kind of relationship corresponds to the sound made by the Sanskrit vowel 'h' *(visarga)*, which when written is depicted as two dots, one over the other. Its numerical value is two. The corresponding relationship that exist between the inner spiritual universe and the outer material universe is one of the primary themes of the *Kalachakra* or Wheel of Time Teaching. The first chapter of this exalted teaching traces, in a veiled manner, the cyclic evolution of the cosmos using astrological symbolism. The second chapter pertains to the direct correspondences that exist between these evolutionary cycles and the individual. Many other analogies are also given, such as correspondences between the nerve centers *(chakras)* within the vajra (etheric) body of the yogi and the centers or chakras of a planetary system. At the beginning of the second chapter Sucandra asks of the Buddha:

> How can the entirety of the three worlds be within the body? Hearing Sucandra's words and applauding him, the Sugata [Buddha], with supreme compassion, expounded the measure of all things within the body, for the sake of liberating sentient beings.[1]

The *Kalachakra Tantra*, along with its famous commentary the *Vimalaprabha*, gives in a symbolic form the primary correspondences that exist between cosmic bodies and currents, earth centers, the spiritual path of the yogi, the energy centers of the etheric body, and certain subtle vibrational frequencies that correspond to and are veiled by, the sounds of the individual letters of the Sanskrit alphabet. For example, Mt. Meru, 'situated at the center of the world,' symbolically

---

[1] 2:1 *Kalacakratantra: The Chapter on the Individual together with the Vimalaprabha.* Translated by Vesna A. Wallace

represents the central magnetic axis of the Earth. It finds an exact correspondence in the central magnetic axis of the human body as well as the central magnetic axis of the solar system. Its vibrational frequency is said to symbolically correspond to the sound of the Sanskrit vowel 'm', which when written is represented by a single dot. (Alice Bailey students might be interested to know that the *Kalachakra Tantra* hints briefly at the correspondence that exists between the Seven Rays, the Seven Planets, and the Seven Rishis of the Great Bear constellation.)[1]

Another example of the natural correspondence that exists between the microcosm and the macrocosm as hinted in the *Kalachakra Tantra* concerns the mythical kingdom of Shambhala 'situated at the top of the world.' Shambhala is to the Earth what the crown chakra is to the vajra [etheric] body of a human being.

The correspondences that exist between life principles, as they manifest in like kind upon each plane, along with their geometric formulas and subtle sound vibrations, remain among the most secret of all the esoteric doctrines. Brother D.K. lists a few of these natural correspondences in his *A Treaties on Cosmic Fire.*

The author of the Agni Yoga Teaching, reverently referred to as the 'Teacher,' said: "Since psychic energy is an energy it will not contradict the laws of physics."[2] This simple statement affirms the fundamental unity of the laws of nature as applied to both the physical and the psychic worlds.

> When climbing a mountain one leaves behind all unnecessary loads. Is it not the same in the spiritual world? A man falling from a height increases speed as he falls and not even the softest mattress will save the falling one. Is it not the same in the spiritual world? One can compare the foundation of all worlds and come to see the uniformity of laws.[3]

---

[1] See Mipham's *A Commentary on the Shambhala Sections of the Kalachakra Tantra.*

[2] *AUM 487*

[3] *Supermundand: The Inner Life.* Book I, *83*

Edwin Babbitt in his outstanding scientific treatise, *The Principles of Light and Color,* also affirms this principle:

> It should be understood that the very same laws rule the spiritual and intellectual phases of being as in the material. In other words, unity of principle rules in every department of the universe and binds the whole in one.[1]

If scientists would apply the law of correspondence to the known laws of physics they might soon discover that thoughts and emotions are in fact substantial yet very subtle forms of energy. Many people instinctively know this when they speak of feeling someone's good or bad 'vibrations.' A useful book could be written correlating the laws of physics with the laws of psychic energy . Telepathy, no matter how well proven according to the existing standards of probability, will not enter the mainstream of science until thought is understood as a subtle form of energy. The strong materialistic bias, so prevalent in the academic community today, is one of the primary obstacles to new discoveries.

That Proclus, who was undoubtedly an initiate of the lesser Mysteries, understood the Law of Analogy as can be seen throughout his writings:

> In the heavens the monad and heptad is in analogy with that of the ethereal sphere, which correspond to the circles of the planets and fixed stars. The whole ethereal sphere imitates the heavens.[2]

According to Proclus, Plato's writings were often veiled in symbolic phrases, which could only be understood by applying the Law of correspondence. Proclus states, for example, that when Plato

---

[1] Edwin Babbitt *Principles of Light and Color.* 1878 (Unabridged edition of 570 pages) page 10. This book is mentioned by Brother D.K. in his *A Treatise on Cosmic Fire,* (page 1182). The common reprint is highly abridged, more than half of it was rejected by the publisher and editor as being unscientific.

[2] Proclus' Commentary on Plato's Dialogues on Nature (Timaeus).

writes of Egypt and the Nile in his *Dialogues on Nature* he is referring to the stream of vital life entering and giving nourishment to the whole world from its source, the constellation of the Bear. This kind of symbolic veiling is true of the writings of nearly all the ancient initiates of both the East and the West. The Vedas, for instance, were written almost entirely in this kind of symbolic code. Because of the very strict vows of silence enforced in all true esoteric schools students could not write openly of the secrets that they had received during initiation or from their teachers. Therefore they often veiled universal principles by presenting them on one level only, leaving it to those students with an awakened intuitive awareness to make the necessary application to other fields. Many of the authentic alchemists, for example, particularly those connected with the Rosicrucians, used truths pertaining to chemistry to represent higher truths pertaining to their natural correspondences in the body, in the world as a whole, in the solar system of planets and in those primordial energies inherent to the generation and evolution of the world. By understanding the exact correspondences that naturally exist between the mineral kingdom and the constitution of a human being the illuminated alchemist could write about the transfiguration of the body into a body of light, the 'wedding garment of the alchemical marriage,' by veiling it as the transmutation of one element into another higher element[1] Once the laws of correspondence are intuitively understood, the hidden meaning behind much of the symbolism of the Mysteries becomes clear.

Paracelsus, the highly accomplished 16th century initiate, alchemist and remarkable healer, developed his worldview based upon the analogies that naturally exist between the divine signatures of the macrocosm and their corresponding reflections in the physical world. Paul M. Allen, in his excellent introduction to Rudolf Steiner's *Mysticism at the Dawn of the Modern Age,* writes of this view:

> One of Paracelsus' most far-reaching concepts is that of Signatures, that is, the idea that each single part of the

---

[1] See my *A Synthesis of Alchemy* Pentarba Publications, 1994..

microcosmic world of man corresponds with each single part of the macrocosm.

Jacob Boehme expanded upon this idea in his *Signature of All Things*. That Isaac Newton, who had studied the writings of Jacob Boehme, also understood the principle of analogy, can be seen in his book, *The Prophecies of Daniel*. He even devoted one of its chapters on how to decipher the symbolic language used in the books of *Daniel* and the *Apocalypse of St. John*.[1]

> For understanding the *Prophecies*, we are in the first place, to acquaint ourselves with the figurative language of the Prophets. This language is taken from the *analogy* between the world natural, and an Empire or Kingdom [of God].[2]

The structure of the 'natural world,' says Isaac Newton, corresponds to the 'Kingdom of Thrones and Powers.' This spiritual Kingdom, he says, is "The hierarchy of spiritual beings that govern the progress of the saints."

Isaac Newton, while primarily known for his material-science writings, was essentially a Hermetic philosopher and alchemist. His surviving manuscripts on alchemy, Hermetic philosophy, Pythagorean science, and occult theology, written in his own hand amount to over 650,000 words. This remarkable lifetime achievement was inspected after his death by prominent members of the Royal Society and marked "not for publication." To this day they have not been made public, even as historical curiosities! Not only were his Hermetic writings censored but so were his scientific writings on hylozoism, the living nature of matter. Newton affirmed along with the Pythagoreans that the planetary bodies were animate rather than inanimate objects. He even postulated that the theory that gravity was due to the livingness of matter. This, of course, went against the scientific dogma

---

[1] *Observations upon the Prophecies of Daniel and the Apocalypse of St. John.* By Isaac Newton Reprinted by Nu Vision Publications 2007

[2] Page 16

of his time and was therefore censored. If these scientific papers had been published it may have completely changed the direction of scientific thinking of his time. Newton is credited with the discovery of gravity and its properties, but according to Newton himself it was Pythagoras who first made the discovery many years before. In his *Notes* intended for the second edition of his *Principia Mathematica,* but not so published, Newton states that Pythagoras discovered the inverse square relationship in vibrating strings; and that he then extended this idea to the corresponding relationships of the weights and distances of the planets from the sun. While Pythagoras kept secret the knowledge of the correspondences that exists between celestial harmonics and music, Newton rediscovered it by studying the writings of the Pythagoreans. The following excerpt from his *Notes* demonstrates that he understood the esoteric teachings on this and could translate them into the scientific language of his day.

So far I have expounded the properties of gravity. Its cause I by no means recount. Yet I shall say that the ancients thought about this subject. Thales regarded all [planetary] bodies as animate, deducing that from magnetic and electrical attractions. And by the same argument he aught to have referred the attraction of gravity to the soul of matter. Hence he taught that all things are full of Gods, understanding by Gods animate bodies. He held the sun and the Planets for Gods. And in the same sense Pythagoras, on account of its immense force of attraction, said that the sun was the prison of Zeus, that is, a body possessed of the greatest circuits. And to the mystical philosophers Pan was a supreme divinity inspiring this world with harmonic ratio like a musical instrument and handling it with modulation, according to that saying of Orpheus 'striking the harmony of the world in playful song.' Thus they named harmony God and the soul of the world composed of harmonic numbers. But they said that the Planets move in their circuits by the force of their own souls, that is, by the force of the gravity, which takes its origin from the action of the soul.[1]

Initiates, we are told, work in all fields of human evolution including the scientific arena. It is known, for example, that Albert Einstein had a copy of H. P. Blavatsky's *The Secret Doctrine* on his desk till the day he died.[2] What is not well known is that he also occasionally borrowed books form the Lucis Trust Library in New York. As their records indicate one of the books he borrowed was the above mentioned *A Treatise on Cosmic Fire.* As to why he would hide his Theosophical leanings we need only quote the Teacher: "Those with daring and acute perceptions must, like the alchemists of old, hide from the inquisition."[3]

Plato, who was a Pythagorean, based his worldview upon the hierarchal principle of correspondence. Throughout his writings he maintained that the essential nature of intelligence is of the spiritual world, that the soul prior to the physical experience lives in the spiritual world, and that the original 'Idea-form' (*eidos*), the archetypal thought-form of an intended manifestation, remains impressed upon the deeper levels of the consciousness even while in physical incarnation. It is because of this, he says, that we can obtain a direct understanding of higher truth simply by elevating the consciousness.

By understanding the seeds, the essential archetypal nature behind the shadowy projection into material form, we can begin to understand its evolution toward perfection. This marks the major distinction between esoteric science and material science. Esoteric science directs its attention toward the cause and source of manifested life. Physical science deals only with their effects. Spiritual science looks for the universal synthesis, the underlining essential unity. The materialists look to the particular, thereby becoming specialists.

---

[1] See Joscelyn Godwin's *The Harmony of the Spheres: A Source book of the Pythagorean Tradition in Music.* Inner Traditions International, 1993, pages 305-308.

[2] This information, which was given by his niece, was later confirmed by the late Dallas Tenbroeck who said that it was seen by him during a visit .

[3] AUM #309

Esoteric science investigates principles. Material science investigates things. Most material scientists believe falsely that the physical plane is the source of life, mind and consciousness.

In the Mysteries it is taught that from the original archetypal vibration, symbolically called the WORD, arise those formative forces that give shape to the mental and material universe. To understand fully, therefore, how cosmic vibrations form images, concepts, and material forms requires a transformation of our thinking process. Instead of attempting to discover causes merely from their effects in the material world as material science attempts to do, we must learn to include in our calculations the concept, even if not yet fully realized, of the original archetype from which the object is formed. In other words we must learn to think holistically.

Rudolf Steiner, an Austrian born initiate of remarkable visionary abilities, in his introduction to the compiled scientific writings of Goethe, which he edited, states:

> Natural science before Goethe was unaware of the essential nature of living phenomena. It simply investigated organisms with regard to the composition of their parts and external characteristics, just as one investigates inorganic phenomena. Consequently, that older science often interpreted details incorrectly and presented them in a false light. Investigation of the particulars themselves cannot, of course, reveal any such error. Interpretive judgments can only be made after we have first understood the organism [as a whole], because the particulars, considered separately, do not contain the principle that explains them. They can be explained only through the nature of the whole, because it is the whole that gives them being and significance.[1]

H. P. Blavatsky makes a similar statement:

---

[1] *Nature's Open Secret: Introductions to Goethe's Scientific Writings.* Translated by John Barns and Mado Spiegler, Anthrosophic Press, 2000, p. 2

To arrive at the macro-cosmical, you must begin by the microcosmical; i.e. you must study Man, the microcosm—in this case as physical science does—inductively, proceeding from particulars to universals. At the same time, however, since a keynote is required to analyze and comprehend any combinations of differentiations of sound, we must never lose sight of the Platonic method, which starts with one general view of all, and descends from the universal to the individual. This is the method of Mathematics—the only exact science that exists in our day.[1]

Proclus, in his commentary on the first book of Euclid's *Elements*, has this to say:

Some sciences are closer to the Truth than others. A science that starts from simpler principles is superior to one whose starting point is more complex. A science that considers causes is superior to one that studies only effects. A science that is concerned with principles perceived by the mind is superior to one that is concerned with objects perceived by the senses.

Esoteric Buddhism takes a similar view. The Vajrayana student is instructed to look for the essential nature behind the manifestation of shadowy phenomena, to look for the primordial Mind behind our illusive and fragmentary thoughts and feelings and to discover our true Buddha-nature behind the illusion of a separate identity. All the great mystics agree; by penetrating to the root source of the natural world we can discover the reality behind it that does not change.

The science of correspondence was taught in many of the ancient schools of religious philosophy. Philo Judaeus, the first century Alexandrian historian and religious scholar, indicates that the science of analogy was used extensively by the Essenes, a spiritual community of which John the Baptist and Jesus of Nazareth were in some degree connected:

---

[1] *Collected Writings* XII, p.517.

In the interpretation of scripture they [the Essenes] indulged greatly in the use of allegory and correspondence, for the Law appeared to them as a living being, the body of which was the letters and words, the soul being the invisible spirit hidden within.

The visionary anonymous author of *On Mankind Their Origin and Destiny* (1872) gives evidence to show that the Essenes were an offshoot of the Mystery Schools of Egypt.

Pythagoras, who like Plato was an initiate of the Egyptian Mysteries, taught his students that the incorporeal unchanging essence of things could and should be approached, but only after the mind had been trained in the sciences, or those laws and principles by which the universe manifests itself into form; namely, music, mathematics, geometry, correspondence and harmony. He taught that in this way we could begin to trace the thread of creation back to its source. He taught that only by degrees should we progress from a study of the parts, to how those parts evolve and are united together, to an eventual understanding of the essential nature or universal synthesis of the One hidden behind it. Maitreya, the future Buddha, in his treatise in verse, *Understanding the Distinction Between the Appearance of Phenomena and Its Essential Nature,* presents this idea from the Buddhist perspective:

It is first essential to perceive the difference between the appearance of phenomena and its essential nature before we can understand that [from a higher perspective] there is no difference between them at all.

In the great *Pranava-Veda: The Science of the Sacred Word* by Gargyayana we read:

Before the jiva [human being] can realize Unity it must first have studied the diversity that is pervaded by that Unity.[1]

1 *The Pranava-vada: The Science of the Sacred Word.* By Gargyayana, translated by Bhagavan Das, in three volumes, Theosophical Publishing 1910. Vol. 1., page 21.

Rudolf Steiner, in his lectures on *The Gospel of Mark,* writes:

> What is important is that we should recognize things in such a way that we look for *both* differentiations and the underlying unity behind them; that we characterize things according to their differences and only afterwards look for the higher unity to be perceived in these differences.

With some exceptions this marks one of the differences that exist between the methods used in the Mystery Schools and those of Mysticism. While ultimately the spiritual goal is the same for both, namely the understanding of our essential nature, the method of approach often differs greatly. In the Mystery-Hermetic culture one develops gradually, step by step, from the rational to the abstract and then on to the higher intuitive faculties. Mystics, on the other hand, often attempt to bypass the rational mind altogether by penetrating in the intuitive consciousness to their essential nature directly. In both cases the rational conceptual mind is eventually transcended through direct firsthand intuitive understanding. In both cases sense perception is bypassed for a time and the thought mechanism stilled so that a higher faculties of perception may be brought into play. For the mystic this faculty is the bodhi-mind or direct insight. For the occultist it is clairvoyance and insight. The transcendence of sense perception so that a higher faculties of perception my come into play is called *Pratyahara*.[1] It is one of the eight limbs of Raja Yoga as is the stilling of the thought mechanism. There is another distinction between occultism and mysticism. The mystic perceives reality. The occultist applies this vision for the fulfillment of the Plan.

Initiates and Mystics are as brothers and sisters on the Path. Many mystics are also initiates and all initiates are mystics. We might note here that that the term 'mystic,' from the Greek *mystikos,* was according to Proclus "the name given to an initiate who had reached the first degree of the Mysteries." The terms 'mystery' and 'mystic'

---

[1] See Patanjali's *Yoga Sutras,* II.54-55.

have the common root 'mythos,' meaning 'to be silent.' In the Mysteries the injunction 'To know, to will, to dare, to be silent' has several progressive levels of meaning, the silence of the tongue, the silence of the senses, the silence of concrete mind and finally the silence of Initiation Itself. In *The Book of Hermes* this mystery is embodied in the ninth book, the *Watchman*, who veils the inner light from the public eye. The term 'myth' has the same root. Many if not most of the world-class myths and legends were originally veiled esoteric teachings given to the public by initiates of the Mysteries in an allegorical form. D.K. says:

> Both ways are seen to be essential; the mystical way is for the majority at this time, and an increasingly large number of mystics will emerge out of the modern masses of men; paralleling this, the occult way is attracting more and more of the world intelligentsia. …. The mystical way leads to the first initiation…. The 'new man' who has come to birth at the first initiation must and will tread the occult or scientific way, which inevitably leads him out of the world of mysticism into the scientific and assured perception of God as life or energy.[1]

The Pythagoreans taught that music, when approached through the law of correspondence, could be an accurate way to understand and express the original archetypal vibrations of the cosmos as they are stepped down through the many octaves of being.[2] According to an esoteric interpretation of some of the early Greek myths the seven-stringed lyre of Apollo represents one of the keys to the seven basic archetypal vibrations originating from the seven sacred planets. Pythagoras made use of this key to express the principles of Nature geometrically. According to the ancient science of Taoism, which according to Rudolf Steiner can be traced clairvoyantly back to the time of Atlantis, the seven archetypal vibrations originate with the

---

[1] *The Rays and the Initiations*, page 666.

[2] See *The Harmony of the Spheres: A Sourcebook of the Pythagorean Tradition in Music* edited by Joscelyn Godwin, Inner Traditions 1993

seven Gods of the Great Bear constellation. The Ancient Chaldeans and Acadians symbolized the universe as being encircled by a great serpent with seven heads representing the seven stars of the Great Bear constellation. This great serpent swims in the crystalline sapphire ocean of the heavens and like the 'golden cord' of Homer, unifies and holds the universe together.[1] In the Vedic Mysteries the seven Gods of the Great Bear constellation are called the 'Seven Rishis.' According to Steiner the 'Seven Rishis' are represented in the Book of Revelations (1:16 & 20) as the 'Mystery of the Seven Stars.'[2] The seven candlesticks represent the lower correspondences of these seven stars as the 'Seven Churches,' the seven great Ashrams of the Hierarchy.

Brother D.K. calls these seven archetypal currents the 'Seven Rays,' which he says "emanate from the seven Rishis of the Great Bear constellation," forming the seven basic archetypes for all manifested life as found in the seven principles, the seven sacred planets, the seven etheric centers in the body, the seven races, the seven planetary periods, the seven esoteric schools (ashrams, churches), the seven planes, and the seven soul qualities, to name a few of the possible correspondences. An important book on the essential nature of beauty

---

[1] Simular to *Adi Shesha*, the celestial seven headed Naga (serpent) of the Hindus, who holds the universe together.

[2] *Reading the Pictures of the Apocalypse.*

in art may someday be written concerning the progressive interaction of these seven fundamental energies and their harmonic expression through color, rhythm, and geometrical form. Johann Sebastian Bach it seems, in some of his latter compositions, experimented with this idea by cryptically encoding some of the musical keys to the mystery of harmonics in relation to the sacred Trinity in his *Six Solos for Unaccompanied Violin.* The Hilliard Ensemble gives a very beautiful demonstration of this in their music CD *Morimur.* In the accompanying booklet to this CD Professor Helga Thoene, who discovered the musical cryptograms, writes a short article called *The Secret Language— Hidden Chorale Quotations in J.S. Bach's 'Sei Solo a Violino.'*

Plato taught that the first principle of music originates from the pure unchanging nature of the Logos or WORD, manifesting as those divine Idea-forms (*Eidos*) that are the true nature and origin of all things. The Greek term 'Eidos' is usually translated into English as either Idea or Form, both of which are accurate as far the term itself is concerned. But as used by Plato in his dialogues it means those divine thought-forms that are the archetype and cause of the manifested world perceived by the senses. Richard Tarnas, in his brilliant treatise on the history of ideas *The Passion of the Western Mind,* defines the Eidos as archetypal principles:

> These archetypal principles include the mathematical forms of geometry and arithmetic; cosmic opposites such as light and dark, male and female, love and hate, unity and multiplicity; the forms of man (*snthopos*) and other living creatures; and the Idea of the Good, the Beautiful, the Just, and other absolute moral and aesthetic values.

Plato speaks of these archetypal thought-forms throughout his writing, but always in a veiled manner. Nowhere does he write plainly on the subject. This is undoubtedly due to the vow of silence that was required of all initiates of the Mystery culture of his time. Plato taught that the supersensible world, the origin of these archetypal principles, was the world of being, while the world of the senses, the world of the materialization of those divine ideas, was the sphere of becoming. This divine becoming, he taught, follows the impulses emanating from the archetypal world. The principles that pertain to humanity's becoming, when voluntarily followed, lead to the world of pure being. These archetypal thought-forms, therefore, are the formulas, the blueprints for humanity's evolution into the higher worlds of close spiritual relationships, pure understanding and being. So say the Initiates. Adrian Snodgrass, in his monumental work, *Architecture, Time and Eternity*,[1] gives a clear allegorical picture of Plato's perspective on this:

> In the allegory of the cave Plato likens the condition of man to that of prisoners chained within a cave so that they cannot move and can only look ahead to the cave wall, on which they see shadows cast by moving puppet-like figures lit by a fire behind them. The prisoners take the shadows to be the only reality. If, however, a prisoner can free himself form his bonds and turn around, he will see the objects whose shadows appear on the cave wall. Walking upwards through the cave he will pass the fire and leave the cave to emerge into the sunlight. At first his eyes will be painfully dazzled and will not be able to perceive the objects whose shadows he had seen upon the cave wall. Gradually, however, as his eyes become accustomed to the light, he will perceive real things in the light of the sun. And finally he may even be able to glance at the sun itself.

The fundamental principles of archetypal symbolism, however, did not originate with Plato, but with the Mysteries into which he had been initiated. It is through the sacred Mysteries, whose influence at one time extended throughout most the known world, both east and west, that the science of archetypal symbolism finds expression as a natural language representing the true name of things, the signature of their essential nature. But as the temple brethren were not allowed to speak or write openly concerning the true nature of this archetypal

---

[1] Volume 1, page 13

language, they had to find other ways in which to preserve and pass on a portion of the these mysteries to the world without 'casting pearls before swine,' without revealing precious secrets to those who would only criticize and distort them. This they did by incorporating the natural and geometric symbols of the Ageless Wisdom in the architecture of their temples, stupas, and cathedrals and by creating allegorical stories (myths), songs and Mystery Plays. It is for this reason that initiates were often called 'Temple Builders' and 'Masons.' The sacred architecture of the most ancient religious traditions, if studied with an understanding of archetypal symbolism, can reveal many of the hidden secrets of creation, evolution, and the 'path of return.'[1]

Plato, whom Proclus called a 'Hierophant of those true Mysteries into which souls, while separated from the terrestrial plane, are initiated,'[2] writes briefly of an intermediate class of symbolic images between the pure archetypal thought-forms (*Eidos*) of the spiritual world and their earthly counterparts. Here he comes close to revealing forbidden secrets and it is no wonder that some of his fellow initiates complained loudly that he was revealing important secrets of the Mysteries to the uninitiated public.[3] Paracelsus hints at this intermediate class of archetypal signatures in his *De Natura Rerum* (1537).

> The divine signatures are threefold. The first depicts the world of man, the second are *archaeus* signs, and the third, originating from the stars, are of a transcendental nature.

According to Rudolf Steiner the term 'archaeus,' so often used by Paracelsus, means etheric (subtle) matter, sometimes the etheric body. Proclus expands somewhat on this intermediate class

---

[1] See *The Symbolism of the Stupa* by Adrian Snodgrass, undoubtedly one of the best books available on true sacred geometry.

[2] This statement from the second page of *The Six Books of Proclus* reveals in only a lightly veiled manner one of the secrets of the Mysteries, namely that initiation takes in the higher worlds. This idea, with which we shall deal shortly, is confirmed by the Apostle Paul, Dionysius the Areopagite, H. P. Blavatsky, Rudolf Steiner, and Brother D.K.

[3] See Manly Hall's the *Secret Teachings of All Ages,* 1927 p. 21.

of symbolic images in his commentary on Plato's *A Dialog on Nature:*

> According to the Pythagorean doctrine, Nature can be understood in a three-fold division—Eidos (Idea-forms), physical things, and the media between them, which is usually represented through mathematics [geometry].... This link manifests directly from the *Eidos* as symbolic images.... Prior to physical things exist the images of their essential nature.... Plato defines the character of these pre-existing images as *geometrical figures*, the origin of which are the Idea-forms (*Eidos*) of divine intelligence.

"Anyone who is able to survey the world of spirit clairvoyantly," says Rudolf Steiner, "can find that there exact images of the great cosmic prototypes." Proclus says that the subtle vibrations of the WORD (*Logos*) manifest as 'geometric images of light.' It is from these archetypal images, seen clairvoyantly by the initiate midway between the divine archetype and its reflection in the world of form, that Sensa, the language of the Gods and Voice of Nature is derived.

The Sufi master Abu Bakr Siraj De-Din informs us that, "Although everything on earth is a more or less direct reflection of a higher reality, it is only the most direct reflections that can be called truly symbolic." The true nature of true symbolism is not arbitrarily devised but rather conforms to the natural law of correspondences and octaves.

Through the language of analogy we can greatly expand our understanding of how the macrocosm, the world of causes, is reflected in the microcosm, the world of effects. And when this understanding is coupled with the harmonics of music, dance, architecture, painting, video a whole new creative art form and science will emerge.

The Language of the Gods

The spiritual world has its own written script and language.
Sepher ha Zohar (The Book of Light)

We have a magic writing, copied from that divine alphabet with which God writes His will upon the face of celestial and terrestrial Nature. *Rosicrucian Confessio Fraternitatis*

A certain language and script is learned by those who have been initiated into the Mystery Schools. All the initiates of the world can write and speak in this symbolic language.
Rudolf Steiner

We contemplate the divine Mysteries by way of the symbols that are naturally attached to them. What is necessary is to uncover these symbols, to see them in their purity.

It is well known to students of the Esoteric Tradition that behind the physical body of any living organism there is an invisible and complex energy field called the etheric body from which it receives its life, quality, rhythm and form. It is also known that these vital bodies are all interconnected and together form the one great etheric web, or energy field, for the planet. This is the foundation upon which the esoteric or hidden side of nature is taught in the genuine Mystery Schools and is generally known by serious students of that tradition.

What is not generally known is that there is another, deeper level to this same truth; that behind nature's invisible energy field lies a united network of very subtle archetypal thought-patterns originating from the spiritual world. In the Mystery Tradition these pure archetypal vibrations, taken as a whole, is symbolically called the 'WORD.' In the west we speak of the 'Lost WORD,' and 'In the beginning was the WORD,' etc. In India this concept is also called the WORD or *Vac* with the same meaning; i.e., the original vibrational impulse behind the creation and evolution of the world, 'the first differentiation of the undifferentiated Brahman.' Plato taught that the WORD *(Logos)* was the expression of the original archetypal Idea-form *(Eidos)* arising from divine Intelligence and that it contains within it, "the fixed patterns that are the true nature of things and of which all things are made in their image and likeness." The Word is a reflection of the Divine Idea.

Origen, undoubtedly the most enlightened of the early Christian Fathers, writes of the two levels on which the Christian Mysteries can be understood, the exoteric and the esoteric:

> To the literal minded we teach the Gospel in the historic way, preaching Jesus Christ and Him crucified; but for the proficient, fired with a love for divine wisdom, we impart the WORD.[1]

---

[1] From his *Introduction to the Book of John*

Clement of Alexandria, an initiate of the lesser mysteries who later became a Christian states:

God permits a portion of the divine Light of the Mysteries to those who can attain it. He does not reveal to the masses what is unsuitable for them. Only to those few who can perceive it within themselves is the unspeakable mystery of God made manifest, not through the written word, but through the WORD.

The hidden meaning behind the lost archetypal WORD remains one of the primary secrets of occultism. The secrecy stems from the fact that it is also one of the keys to the science of magic, which in the wrong hands is dangerous. H.P. Blavatsky, while veiling nearly all her writings concerning the hidden or lost Word, clearly states in the back pages of her *Theosophical Glossary* that *Vach* or WORD "represents in one sense the 'secret mystic speech' of the Rishis." Rudolf Steiner affirms this idea:

The geometrical and symbolic figures employed as the sacred signs of the great religions are in fact the characters of the creative language of the WORD, the living hieroglyphs of cosmic speech.[1]

According to Blavatsky the 'secret mystic speech,' the symbolic 'Language of the Gods,' was called by the Magi of ancient Persia. 'Sensar, the Language of the Sun,'[2] also spelled Sena, Sensa, Senzar, Zenzar and Zendzar. To the initiates of the Sacred Mysteries the sun is an accurate symbol for the Spiritual Sun, the root Source of all manifested life. Initiates are often called 'Children of the Sun,' The WORD is considered to be the root vibration or keynote of the Spiritual Sun. "The Great Work," says Hermes, "is the work of the Sun." The ancient Egyptians called the characters of their hieroglyphs 'images of the sun.' The Oracle of Apollo declared the Sun to be 'the

[1] 53, p. 78-79
[2] *Isis Unveiled*, 1877, Vol. 1, page 440

king of the seven sounded harmonies."[1] From the ancient Egyptian pyramid texts we learn that "from the mouth of Piope [Osiris of the Sun] came forth both the great WORD  and Sena

". There is some evidence to suggest that the Egyptian 'Sena' is closely related to the Arabic 'Sima,' which means a symbolic sign, character or image. The Sufi master Ibn 'Arabi writes:

> The term 'simiya,' which is derived form the Arabic *'sima*,' means the science of symbolic images in which magical effects are produced by combining certain letters, names and words. Some people have received an understanding of this science merely by (repeating) the Name of God. It is the source of the magical practices of the Pharaohs.[2]

The Sufis taught that the creative science of symbolic images (*simiya*) and the science of analogy and correspondence (*'ilm al-mathan*) are both expressions of the WORD. The Sufi term *'nuskha'* concerns the symbolism of letters as they relate to the perfect correspondence that exists between the spiritual world and the material world, between God and man. According to the Sufis the science of letters, signs, and correspondence is expressed in secret through an esoteric language called the *Ta'wil,* or Hidden Tongue. The exoteric meaning of this term refers to the hidden meaning (*batin*) behind the usual literal interpretation (*zahir*) of the scriptures, which acts as a veil hiding the inner truth from the general public. The secret meaning of the term refers to a secret language of signs and symbols. The *Ta'wil* is closely connected with the science of Divine Names, which is said to awaken the spiritual vision of the divine lights. Hidden within the sounds of

---

[1] See the Pythagorean Euseoius' *Preparation of the Gospel,* Book 1, chapter 22.

[2] *al-Futuhat al-makkiya* II 135.28-29

divine names lie the symbolic depictions of spiritual principles and laws. Idries Shah, in his book *The Sufis*, has this to say about the ta'wil:

> It has the advantage of connecting mundane thinking with the greater dimensions, the 'other world' from which ordinary humanity is cut off.... The secret language, because it is not only a cipher to prevent the profane form understanding things with which they cannot correctly attune themselves, and because it is thought to connect with a greater reality, is immensely complicated in effect. It is the subject of Sufi study in the circles of the teachers, and once its method of procedure is understood, at least one layer of its working is revealed.[1]

Henry Corbin, the brilliant esoteric interpreter of Sufi literature, states:

> The *Ta'wil* is essentially that symbolic understanding that intuitively transmutes everything visible into its symbolic essence-image, that partakes neither of logic nor sense perception, and is the only [true] means by which it can be signified...[2]
>
> A symbol is not an artificially created sign; it spontaneously flowers in the soul indicating something that cannot be expressed otherwise. It is the unique expression of that which is being symbolized, as a reality that thus becomes transparent to the soul, but which in itself transcends all expression.[3]

Elsewhere, drawing from the writings of Ibn 'Arabi, he states that the Ta'wil has 'seven levels of esoteric meaning embodied by the seven prophets of eternal Being.' Ibn 'Arabi says that these seven levels or planes correspond to the seven Archangels and the seven planets. Blavatsky says that the 'seven prophets' etc. correspond to the

---

[1] p. 195

[2] *Creative Imagination in the Sufism of Ibn 'Arabi.* Henry Corbin, Princeton Univ. Press, 1981, page 13.

[3] *Avicenna and the Visionary Recital,* by Henry Corbin, page 30, Spring Publications, 1980.

seven Dhyani Buddhas, who embody for humanity the seven primordial prototypes of our spiritual evolution.[1]

In the *Book of Light (Sepher ha Zohar)*, the primary source work of the Hebrew Kabbalah, it is said that the divine WORD of creation is expressed through a secret language called the Holy Tongue (*Leshon Hakodesh*). This holy tongue, says, Rabbi Simeon, 'is spoken by the heavenly host.'

> The spiritual kingdom has its own written script and language. None of the nations of the world possess this language or its script because of their vanity and delusion. Their language is based upon arbitrarily agreed upon forms, language, and script. Those who think in these [arbitrary] letterforms do not possess the true script. [Therefore] they shall not understand its secrets.... The Holy Tongue acts as a bridge carrying the *creative currents* of the spiritual world to the material plane. Hidden within the shape of its letters the secrets of creation are revealed.

There is *ample* evidence throughout *The Book of Light* that this 'lost and forgotten,' language that was 'taught to Joseph by an angel' and that 'none of the nations possess,' is not Hebrew or Armenian, as some commentators seem to believe, though there are undoubtedly correspondences in the sounds and perhaps, in a few cases, even in the shape of its letters. Part of the confusion may have arisen from the fact that Hebrew is also called the 'holy tongue.' But the 'Holy Tongue,' spoken of in the *Book of Light*, is the one magical language that was *lost* after the fall of the Tower of Babel, due to its misuse.

> One of the chief characteristics of the Holy Tongue is that it enables everyone to express themselves clearly and unmistakably in terms exactly corresponding to their thoughts, wishes, and intentions, and that it is understood and comprehended by the forces of nature, who when hearing it are impelled to assist and help those who utter it.

---

[1] There are five exoteric and seven esoteric Dhyani Buddhas.

From the *Book of Light* we learn that a form of this sacred language was taught to Adam by one of the Elohim and that it was then passed down in the *Book of Adam* through the initiate prophets, until the time of the Tower of Babel, at which time its creative potency, made powerful through group use, was so badly misused that not only were those who were misusing it 'scattered over the face of the earth,' but 'the very names of the creative forces were changed' to prevent the elemental forces of nature from responding. The Tower of Babel symbolizes the Atlantean civilization under the reign of the dark magicians. Its fall, like the Falling Tower hieroglyph in the *Book of Hermes* (another name for the *Book of Adam*) was necessary to the evolution of humanity.[1]

> It is the Atlantean civilization, which is symbolized by the Tower of Babel, a civilization whose base rested upon the earth but whose top reached into the higher realms, farther than man of that day was entitled to go.[2]

"And they said let us make a city and a tower whose top may reach to heaven and let us make ourselves a name."[3] The *Book of Light* says that 'the city and tower' symbolically represent the two higher worlds, Yesod and Malkut, which were then accessible to the followers of evil. Apparently the Holy Tongue gave them direct access to the astral and lower mental planes. This and the name or keynote they had created for themselves through the Holy Tongue gave them great power upon the physical plane. The fall of the Tower of Babel, the destruction of Atlantis, ended this ability.

> Thus, their language was confounded and they were no longer able to strengthen their inventions. The subtle powers and entities [elemental forces] know only the spiritual language, so when this language was lost their strength failed and their power

---

[1] See *The Book of Hermes,* Pentarba Publications 2018.
[2] See *The Voice of Isis* by H. Curtiss page 237.
[3] Genesis 11:14

was broken.... Because of the dispersion of the humans involved, the true science of words and sounds was lost, but not irretrievably so. In the ages to come it will be recovered once again, creating thereby a greater union and harmony between heaven and earth, between the angels and humanity, and between all the nations and peoples of the world. The Holy Tongue, lost and forgotten, will be spoken again in all its purity, and the prophecies found in the sacred scriptures will be fulfilled.

The *Book of Light (Zohar)* tells us that even after the fall of the Tower of Babel the Holy Tongue continued to be passed down through the prophets Noah, Abraham, Moses, Solomon, etc. Rudolf Steiner says that this 'Lost Archetypal Word,' as he calls it, finally disappeared in the 'fourth post-Atlantean period' at the time of transition from the predominance of Greek culture to Roman-Latin culture. Veiled legends concerning the 'Lost Word' (or language) have been preserved in Masonry and elsewhere, along with the prophecy that it would be recovered again when humanity was ready to accept responsibility for its use. According to Manly Hall and other esoteric writers the Lost Word will be recovered during the coming 'Resurrection of the Mysteries.' Rudolf Steiner and Alice Bailey, have both written extensively concerning the coming restoration of the Mysteries. In volume 1 of *A Treaties on the Seven Rays* the following symbolic prophecy concerning the restoration of the Mysteries of Initiation and recovery of the Lost Word.

> When the fourth ray and the seventh ray come into incarnation together, we shall have a most peculiar period of revelation and of light bringing. It is said of this time that 'the temple of the Lord will take on an added glory and the Builders will rejoice together.' This will be the high moment of the Masonic work, spiritually understood. The Lost Word will then be recovered and uttered for all to hear, and the Master will arise and walk

among His builders in the full light of the glory that shines from the east.[1]

The 'Rays,' spoken of here, are the seven archetypal currents that descend from the higher worlds providing the impulse and keynote for humanity's spiritual growth along certain predetermined lines. These Rays are cyclic in nature entering the field of manifestation and influence with greater intensity at set periods. The 'Seventh Ray,' which pertains to economics, organization, rhythm, and the manifestation and utilization of subtle energies, is now beginning to make its presence felt. 'The Fourth Ray,' which deals with the principle of harmonics, beauty and art through the unity and balance of the pairs opposites, will begin to make its appearance, D. K. tells us, after the year 2025. 'The Masonic work, spiritually understood' refers to the true Mysteries and not any outer organization. 'His builders,' are those working to further the Great Work of Evolution. 'The temple of the Lord will take on an added glory' and 'the full light of the glory which shines from the east,' refers to the spiritualization of the new form or temple that the outer manifestation of the Great Lodge, the spiritual Hierarchy, will take, through a closer more exact alignment with the divine Archetype, or WORD. 'The Master will arise and walk among His builders,' means an externalization of the spiritual Hierarchy of Masters who guides the spiritual evolution of the world and the restoration of the Sacred Mysteries of Initiation. The Lost Word will then be recovered and uttered for all to hear,' means that the Language of the Gods will, to some extent, be made public. It is with this purpose in mind that the present treatise has been written. The Lost Word, though single in essence, manifests as a multidimensional language sounded out as vibrating light images and thought-forms vibrant with meaning, creativeness, and evolutionary purpose.

At a certain point on the Path all initiates learn a portion this 'esoteric script.' Each initiation, we are told, takes the initiate a step closer to mastering it completely. It is through this archetypal language

---

[1] Pages 52-53.

that the greater secrets of initiation are given. Rudolf Steiner clarifies this process somewhat in his highly informative book, *How to Gain a Spiritual Perception of the Higher Worlds*:

> If, having completed the 'trial by fire,' we decide to continue the Path of Initiation, then a particular system of writing, customarily used in occult training, is unveiled to us. The characters of this script reveal the actual secret teachings. For what is really 'hidden' in things is not directly expressible in the words of ordinary language, nor recordable in any ordinary system of writing.... This occult language is inscribed forever in the spiritual world. Once the soul has attained spiritual perception the language is revealed to it. But we do not learn to read this occult alphabet in the same way that we learn to read an ordinary human alphabet. Rather, it is as if we grow toward clairvoyant knowing, and while we grow, there develops in us (as a faculty of the soul) a force impelling us to decipher, as if they were the characters of a language, the events and beings the spiritual world presents before us.... The signs of this occult language are not arbitrarily devised but correspond to forces at work in the world. As candidates for initiation we realize immediately that these signs correspond to the figures, colors, and sounds that we learned to perceive in the earlier stages of preparation and illumination.... Now for the first time regular communication between the candidate and other initiates, concerning the realms of higher knowledge, becomes possible.

And in another place in the same book Steiner states:

> Once we have developed the above-described qualities to a certain extent, we are ready to learn the *true names* of things. These names are the key to higher knowledge. Initiation is learning to call the things of this world by the names as they exist in the minds of their divine creators. These names contain the secret nature of these things. Initiates speak a different language

than those who have not been initiated. Initiates speak the true names of things, the names by which they were created.[1]

The subtle sound emanating from the essential nature of a plant, lets say, is its true name. Visually, as viewed by a clairvoyant seer, this subtle sound takes form as distinctive and most beautiful geometric patterns.

In the *Crata Repoa*,[2] a curious 1657 compilation of information by initiates concerning initiation into the Mysteries, we learn of a secret language that is progressively taught to the initiates during each initiation. At the first initiation the Neophyte is 'taught a symbolical language of common hieroglyphic writing.' At the second initiation the Neocaris 'is taught the nature and use of geometry and architecture.' At the third initiation, the Melanephoris 'is taught a particular alphabet named Hierogrammatical, which was useful to the understanding of geometry, astronomy, and the history of Egypt.' At the fourth initiation 'the Initiate is taught the Ammonitish language.' At the sixth initiation 'he is taught the Priestly Dance, the figures of which are based on the course of the stars.' At the seventh initiation 'the Prophet is given the key to all the mysterious books that were written in the Ammonitish language, along with permission to read them.'

The term 'Hiero-grammatical' literally means Language of the Sun. The 'Ammonitish language' pertains to the secret word of the first degree or 'Amoun,' which means 'to be silent.'[3] The third degree of the Mysteries is here called the 'Gate of Death' for 'in the presence of the King Himself'[4] the candidate simulates death, and by leaving his body for several days (some say 3 ½ days) he is guided to the 'mountain top' of initiation (the mental plane) by advanced initiates.

---

[1] The last paragraph of chapter 2
[2] See *Freemasonry of the Ancient Egyptians* by Manly Hall, pages 81-101
[3] Also see Plutarch's *Isis and Osiris*.
[4] The Lord of the World

According to Rudolf Steiner what the initiate learns there is retained in his memory upon reentering the body.[1]

According to this and other reliable esoteric sources the language of the Mysteries is given to the initiate at each initiation in a progressive step-by-step manner. H.P. Blavatsky, in an article written for *La Revue Theosophique* in Paris, relates that while certain numerical values of the mystery-language were taught in the 'Lesser Mysteries' (the first two degrees), "the language itself was reserved for the higher initiates alone. The candidate must have come out victorious from the terrible trials of the Great Mysteries [3rd and up] before receiving instruction in it."[2] Elsewhere Blavatsky states that during initiation one 'receives the WORD.'[3] This is confirmed in the Bailey Books where it is stated that during initiation the WORD becomes both audible and visible. Blavatsky in her *Secret Doctrine* gives one of the tests that the candidate must pass before of taking a certain initiation:

> Every student had to record [a certain event] in corresponding symbols, drawn from his own mind and examined later by his master, before he was finally accepted.[4]

Albert Pike, while writing extensively on initiation and the Mysteries gives only a couple of sentences on the secret 'Language of the Hierophants,' which is taught to the initiate during initiation under very strict vows of silence:

> Initiation was considered to be a mystical death, a descent into the infernal regions, where every pollution, and the stains and imperfections of a corrupt and evil life were purged away by fire and water, and the perfect Epopt [Seer] was then said to be regenerated, new-born, restored to a renovated existence of life, light, and purity, and placed under divine protection. A new

---

[1] See Steiner's *Initiation, Eternity and the Passing Moment.* Anthroposophic Press 1980.

[2] This article was translated into English and appears in her Collected Writings, Vol. XI.

[3] *The Secret Doctrine*, Adyar edition, Vol. 5, p.271

[4] Adyar edition, vol. 2, page 19

language was adapted to these celebrations and also a language of hieroglyphics, unknown to any but those who had received the highest Degree.[1]

John Heydon, a student of the Rosicrucians, in his *Wise Man's Crown,* written in 1664, writes:

> In the *Temple of Wisdom* you see obscure figures of Astrology and Geomancy, wherein is added the alphabet of Angels, writing of the Language of Heaven, affording compendious words partly by stars and characters set in the manner of a wheel. ... Concerning these secrets, my ingenious disciple, if it were lawful to tell you I would.

D.K. in his book *Initiation: Human and Solar,* gives a few hints concerning the secrets of Initiation which are whispered to the Neophyte in the symbolic language of the Mysteries.

> Each secret concerns one or other of the seven great planes of our solar system... Each secret deals with, and is the *enunciation* of, one of the seven laws of Nature.... Each secret concerns some one ray or colour and gives the number, note, and the vibration that corresponds. These seven secrets are simply short formulas, not of mantric value, such as in the case of the sacred word, but of a mathematical nature, precisely worded so as to convey the exact intent of the speaker. To the uninitiated they would look and sound like algebraic formulas, except that each is composed (when seen clairvoyantly) of an oval of a specific hue, according to the secret imparted, containing five peculiar hieroglyphics or symbols. One symbol contains the formula of the law concerned, another gives the planetary key and tone, a third deals with vibration, whilst the fourth shows the number and department under which the ray concerned falls. The hieroglyph gives one of the seven hierarchical keys.... As in the

---

[1] *Morals and Dogma,* page 373

case of the Words...the secret is both heard and appears symbolically to the inner eye.... These formulas are based upon nine symbols that are now recognized:

1. The cross in its varying forms.

2. The lotus.

3. The triangle.

4. The cube.

5. The sphere and the point.

6. Eight animal forms, the goat, the bull, the elephant, the man, the dragon, the bear, the lion, and the dog.

7. The line.

8. Certain signs of the Zodiac...

9. The cup or Holy Grail.

All these symbols allied, interwoven, or taken in part are combined to express one or other of the seven Secrets.[1]

The term 'now recognized,' used above, implies that other symbols that are symbols may also apply. In another place in the same book our Brother has this to say concerning the use of the Sensa language during initiation:

The Oath of Initiation with which we are dealing now is divided into three sections, and is administered by the Hierophant to the initiate, being repeated after the Initiator phrase by phrase; it is punctuated at various points by chanting, by initiates of the same degree, of words in Sensa equivalent to 'So let it be."[2]

'So mote it be' is the phrase is used in Masonry, which is similar in meaning to the Amen used by Christians and the Aum of the Hindus. In the Gnostic *Book of the Great Logos,* we find reference to the Mystery Language as used in the secret 'Baptism of Life,' an initiation ceremony said to have been given by the Christ to his disciples. G.R.S.

---

[1] pages 165 & 166

[2] Pages 146-147.

Mead gives a summary of this initiation ceremony in his *Fragments of a Faith Forgotten:*

> He next seals their foreheads with a certain seal (the diagram of which, authentic name, and interpretation of it—also in the secret cipher—are given).... He then offers a prayer, which is prefixed with an invocation in the mystery-language, interspersed with triple Amens.[1]

Ralston Skinner in his important esoteric treatise, *The Hebrew-Egyptian Mystery* writes of what he calls 'the language of the world:'

> The writer is quite certain that there is an ancient language, which up to this time appears to be lost, the vestige of which, however, abundantly exists... The peculiarity of this language was that it could be contained in another, concealed and not to be perceived, save through the help of special instruction; letters and syllabic signs possessing at the same time the powers or meaning of numbers, of geometrical shapes, pictures, or ideographs and symbols, the designed scope of which would be determinatively helped out by parables in the shape of narratives or parts of narratives; while also it could be set forth separately, independently, and variously, by pictures, in stone work, or in earth construction.[2]

According to Rudolf Steiner the Mystery language, or 'Tau-script' as he sometimes called it, was first discovered by Methusael,[3] of the line of the 'Sons of the Elohim,'[4] which, he says, is of a different evolutionary line than the Sons of Adam.[5]

---

[1] Page 525

[2] Quoted by Blavatsky in her *Secret Doctrine*, Adyar edition, vol. 2, page 20.

[3] *Genesis* 4:18

[4] Also called the Children of Cain. Blavatsky called them the Failures of the Moon Chain.

[5] See Steiner's *

And how actually was this picture-script brought about? The most important signs were taken, not from animal or earthly forms, but from the star-constellations, from what clairvoyance saw in the star-constellations.

Sensa is a visible and audible depiction of the vibrational activity of the laws of nature. The source of these laws, these vibrational patterns, must be looked for in the evolution of the Cosmos and by correspondence the evolution of the consciousness. For this a study of astrology from the perspective of evolution is useful as long as we remember that the usually accepted time calculations are no longer accurate. Due to the procession of equinoxes, which moves forward 1° every 71 years, and the fact that western astrological ephemeris' remain fixed, "the sun is really not in Leo, for instance, during the month of August."[1]

Although reference to this arcane language is rare due to the veil of secrecy that surrounds it (even the existence of the language was generally kept secret) traces of it can be found in the myths, legends, and esoteric teachings of many cultures. The Goddess Minerva, for example, is said to have taught the 'Language of the Birds' to the prophet Tiresias, who in turn passed it on to the great Apollonius of Tyana.[2] The term 'birds,' is often used as a symbol for angelic like spiritual beings or gods. Among the legends of ancient Greece we find the symbolic story of how the Argonauts used a secret language to aid them in their quest for the Golden Fleece, a veiled symbol for the luminous body. Porphyry, the illustrious disciple of Plotinus, in his *Life of Pythagoras* states:

In Egypt he [Pythagoras] lived with the priests and learned their language, wisdom and three kinds of letters, the epistolographic, hieroglyphic and symbolic. One imitates the common way of

[1] *A Treatise on White Magic*, page 437.

[2] See *The Nuctemeron of Apollonius of Tyana Explained by J. Van Rijckenborgh.*

speaking, while the others express a sense of allegory and parable.[1]

Fabre d'Olivet, in his *The Hebraic Tongue Restored,* says:

> Moses, in his teaching, followed the method of the Egyptian priests, who made use of three methods to express their thoughts. The first was the common use. The second was symbolical or figurative. The third was sacred or hieroglyphic... According to their will the same word had the ordinary, figurative and the allegorical meaning. Heraclitus has expressed this difference in three terms, namely the spoken word, the symbol and the hidden meaning.

Cyrano de Bergerac, who Fulcanelli[2] calls a 'great initiate,' gives the following account of the Language of Nature in his L'Autre Monde: Histoire Comique Etats et Empires du Soleil (The Other World: Comic History, States, and Empires of the Sun).

> I do not remember if I spoke to him first or if he was the one who questioned me; but I have a very fresh memory, as if I were still hearing him, of how he talked to me for three long hours in a language which I know I had never heard and which bears no relationship with any language of this world, but which I understand more quickly and more intelligibly than that of my wet nurse. He explained to me, when I inquired about such a marvelous thing [this language was], that "in the sciences there is a truth, which we always fail to see when we move away from simplicity, and that the more a language strayed from this truth the more it went below our understanding. Similarly, in music this truth is never encountered without our soul, being immediately elevated. We don't see it exactly, but we sense that

---

[1] *The Pythagorean Sourcebook and Library*, translated by K. S. Guthrie, Phanes Press, 1988, page 125.
[2] Fulcanelli is the author of the alchemical classic *The Mystery of the Cathedrals* and *The Dwelling of the Philosophers*.

Nature sees it. Even without being able to understand how it absorbs us, we cannot but delight in it, although we do not know its origin. It is the same thing with languages. Whoever encounters this truth of letters, of words, and of continuity can never, while expressing himself, fall below conception: his speech is always equal to his thoughts; and because you do not have knowledge of this perfect language, you do not know what to say, not knowing the order or the words which could express what you imagine". I told him that the first man of our world indubitably used this language, since each name that he imposed on each thing declared its essence. He interrupted me and continued: "This language is not simply necessary to express everything that the mind conceives, but without it we cannot be understood by all. Since this language is the instinct or the voice of Nature, it must be understandable by everything that lives in the midst of Nature. This is why, if you knew it, you could communicate and disclose all your thoughts to the animals, and the animals to you all of theirs, because it is the very language of Nature by which she makes herself understood by all animals. Therefore be no longer surprised by the ease with which you understand the meaning of a language, which your ears have never heard. When I speak, your soul encounters the Truth that it is looking for within each one of my words. And although reason cannot understand it, it has deep within its nature that which cannot but understand it

P. Christian in his remarkable *Histoire de la Magie et du Monde Surnaturel* (*History of Magic and the World of the Supernatural*) published in Paris in 1870, states that 'symbolic writing' and its 'application through the seven keys of symbolism revealed by Hermes' was taught by the initiates of the Egyptian Mysteries. He also states, quoting Iamblichus, that the Egyptian hall where the candidate was tested and prepared for initiation was illustrated with symbolic paintings, which contained that which the magi has received form Hermes-Thoth, 'the great revealer.'

The Sacerdotal knowledge was inscribed above each painting; but only the initiates, to whom the Hierophant confided the key to the mysterious alphabet, which they were sworn to keep secret, could read them.[1]

Jacob Boehme, in his *Aurora* says:

The Language of Nature is the root or mother of all languages that are in this world. In it stands the perfect knowledge of all things…. It is the language of the whole, universal nature. It is not known to everyone for it is a hidden mystery.[2]

In his *The Three Principles of Divine Essence*, he states that he once asked the Divine Mother to teach him the Language of Nature. She refused, but later, he tells us, he learned it very well. "It was imparted to me," says Boehme, "by a spirit who had good feelings toward me." This secret language, he says, 'was taught in the School of Miracles.' In his *Epistles* he says "The Language of Nature has been made known to me so that [through it] I may understand the Greater Mysteries." He goes on to say that in this language the sacred name of Christ signifies 'a powerful champion who shines light into the darkness.'

I certify that the Language of Nature is true, but what I understand of it I cannot teach or give to another. I can only give some indication of it and how it is to be understood, but this would require a lot of space and there must already be an affinity with it in the mind of the student. It is not to be set down in writing.

And in his *Signature of All Things* Jacob Boehme writes:

Therefore the greatest understanding of man lies in his signature, the image of the greatest virtue, whereby he may not only learn

[1] Vol 1, page 114. Also see my *Book of Hermes*.
[2] 20: 88 & 89.

to know himself, but therein also he may learn to know the essence of all essences; for Nature has given signs to everything whereby they are known [to the seer]. This is the Language of Nature, which signifies for what everything is good for. In this lies the mystery and central science of the highest philosophical works and the true healing arts. It indicates a cure not only for the body, but for the soul as well. Everything has its own mouth to manifestation by which it speaks of its own qualities and properties in the Language of Nature.[1]

The divine signatures of things has been used in healing. Paracelsus, for example, could determine the essential nature and purpose of plants by reading their subtle signs. Plutarch, in his *The Mysteries of Isis and Osiris* says:

> There are sacred symbols, some obscure and others less so, that guide the intelligence toward the Mysteries of the Gods, though not without some risk.... Mystic symbols are well known by those of us who belong to the Brotherhood.

To the ancient Greek and Chaldean philosophers these sacred symbols, which they called 'sunthemata,' represented the signatures of the Gods. And as the Gods were believed to be the origin and prototype of all natural things so these symbols were considered to represent by reflection the true names of things. Proclus, who had access to the extensive, but now lost, esoteric writings of the initiate Iamblichus, states in his *The Divine Art of Theurgy* that the Gods could be invoked through their appropriate symbols (*sunthemata*). This was called Theurgy, which P. Christian, the occult historian, defines as "the art of establishing contact with the invisible powers that bridge the distance between God and man through the practice of secret rites." Iamblichus defines Theurgy thus:

---

[1] *Signature of all things*, chapter one.

Of the works of Theurgy performed on any given occasion, some have a cause that is secret and superior to all rational consideration, others are produced through symbols, which have been consecrated from all eternity to the higher beings, others preserve some other image, even as nature in its generative role imprints visible forms from invisible thought forms.[1]

Initiation into the Mysteries is Theurgy at its highest and most secret level of practice. Each initiation, says Proclus, brings the initiate one step closer to complete unification with the Gods and the spiritual principles that they embody. According to Iamblichus, theurgy makes use of "the sacred names of the Gods as well as those divine symbols that have the capacity of raising us up to the Gods and linking with them. [2] When symbols that accurately represent certain higher principles are visualized it creates an invisible link with those principles. To facilitate this, these symbols were sometimes molded from those natural substances that have an affinity with the higher powers or principles being invoked. Proclus explains:

The masters of the divine art of theurgy found a way to serve the Gods by mixing those substances together that have the same qualities of the God [they wished to invoke]. These substances were mixed together because individually they were not strong enough to invoke the Gods. By mixing together different substances they were able to unify the emanations and by the creation of one substance from many they were able to create a likeness of the [archetypal] monad, which existed before its manifestation into form. They created images and incense from these mixtures by forming them into symbols (*sunthemata*), thereby making by art that which a God embodies in essence. They unified the multiplicity of powers, which when dispersed are weak, but when unified lead back up to the essence of the

1 *On the Mysteries* 1: 11
2 *On the Mysteries* 1: 12.

Archetypal Form.... Thus they came to know the powers of those spiritual beings that are essentially linked to the activities of nature and physical bodies. By this they invoked these powers in order to communicate with them. From the Daemonic powers they move up towards the activity of the Gods, sometimes instructed by the Gods themselves, and sometimes through their own efforts they obtained the appropriate symbols. And finally laying aside the physical they obtained unity with the Divine Powers.

The *Chaldean Oracles* of Zoroaster speaks of the divine symbols (*sunthemata*) that were used in the act of creation.

The paternal Mind creates by drawing the Sacred Fire down into matter through the use of symbols, then returning it once again to the divine Order from which it came. This is done through the action and unifying qualities of sacred speech.

The Rishis of ancient India also used geometric symbols to invoke the spiritual energy currents of the Gods. It was possible, they taught, to unite the consciousness with the wisdom energy of certain deities by meditating upon the corresponding geometric patterns that naturally belonged to them. They called these patterns *Yantras*. An example of this can be found in the secret Lonchen Nyingthig practice of esoteric Buddhism.

In the esoteric works of the ancient Hebrew-Chaldean tradition the sacred images, that were said to facilitate contact with the Gods, were created according to their 'inner likeness.' These images were called teraphs or teraphims. They were created either of physical substance or of the astral light through visualization, which is said to be more powerful. In either case the unified substance is magnetized by a reverent saturation of psychic energy.

According to Iamblichus and Proclus the signs and symbols that constitute the Language of the Gods were revealed to those who were initiated into the greater Mysteries. Blavatsky says that Ragon, the 19th century French Mason and author of *Maconnerie Occulte* (*Occult Masonry*) had "certainly studied the Mystery Language."[1] Ragon writes briefly in that work concerning the secret 'Language of the Hierophants' that is communicated to the initiate by the Hierophant during the rite of initiation.[2]

The Teacher and author of the Agni Yoga Books speaks of the 'sacred language,'[3] the 'language of the subtle world,'[4] and the 'eternal language.'[5]

> One need not smile at our Language of the East, the symbols [of which] embody *a complex description of the properties of matter*. We see no need of withholding a brief hieroglyph intelligible to hundreds of people; the more so since these brief signs are beautiful…[6] In our abode, we value the ability to speak briefly. Such hieroglyphs are clearly outlined in space.[7]

They are called 'brief' because the 'symbols,' 'hieroglyphs' and 'signs' flash so quickly and unexpectedly before the mind's eye. They are 'beautiful' because they directly express the laws and principles of

---

[1] Le Phare de L'inconnu. *La Revue Theosophique*, Paris, Vol. 1, 1989

[2] For information on Esoteric Masonry I highly recommend two works *The Spirit of Masonry*, written D.K. and Foster Bailey. And *The Temple Legend* 20 lectures by Rudolf Steiner.

[3] Leaves of Morya's Garden II, # 119

[4] *Fiery World* II, # 283

[5] *Leaves of Morya's Garden* II, III: III,13

[6] *Community* # 224

[7] *Supermundane* # 160

Nature. They are beautiful because "the figures are founded on true cosmic proportions."[1]

It may have been this archetypal language that the initiate Paul heard during his visionary experience (initiation) on the road to Damascus.

> I knew a man of Christ over fourteen years ago, whether in the body or out of the body I cannot say; God knoweth… He was taken up into Paradise, and heard unspeakable words, which it is not lawful for a man to utter.[2]

Later passages indicate that he was speaking of himself in the third person. The phrase 'I cannot say,' and 'it was not lawful for man to utter,' may mean that his vow of silence concerning initiation prevented him from speaking openly upon the subject. Initiation takes place 'out of the body,' which is the true meaning of the seemingly scandalous veiled statement quoted by opponents of occultism, that before initiation into the Mysteries the candidates are required to remove their garments. This veiled statement and the fact that the candidates for initiation were often tested by the opportunity to engage sensual pleasures has contributed the false idea that initiation into the Mysteries consists of orgies of the flesh. In the Mystery community the term 'garment' is often used as a 'blind' or symbol for the physical body, which is discarded in sleep, death, and initiation. St. Paul, in his *Epistles,* again speaks of the 'wisdom tongue:'

> *We* speak *wisdom* among the perfect or *initiated,* not the wisdom of this world, nor of the ministers of this world, but divine wisdom in *mystery* and in *secret,* which none of the ministers of this world know.

---

[1] *Rosicrucian Wisdom* by Rudolf Steiner, page 164

[2] 2 *Corinthians* 12:1-4

By using the terms 'we' and 'initiated' Paul gives us a hint as to his status. Brother D.K. and Rudolf Steiner both say that Paul was an initiate.

Rudolf Steiner informs us that the language of creation or 'stellar script,' as he sometimes called it, was first given to the initiates of the Egyptian Mysteries by the great Hierophant Hermes Trismegistus. This occurred, he says, at a point in evolution where to the Indian quest for a direct understanding of reality was added knowledge of how and why that reality is reflected as the physical universe.

> It was necessary that through initiation the pupil should perceive the Gods. It was also necessary that he should see how the Gods moved their hands in writing the starry script and how all physical forms were thus evolved. While the ancient Egyptians had schools that were entirely based upon the model of the Indians, they also learned how the spiritual forces corresponded with the physical world. Thus they taught new subjects. In ancient India the pupil was shown how the spiritual forces could be perceived through clairvoyance, but in Egypt he was also shown the correspondences that exist between physical and spiritual activity. He was shown how every member of the physical body corresponded to some spiritual labor, how the heart, for example, corresponded to some spiritual work. The founder of this school, in which was shown not only the spiritual but also its work upon the physical, was the great initiator, Hermes Trismegistus. It was he, the thrice-great Thoth, who first showed to men the entire physical world as the handwriting of the Gods.

Manly Hall, in his *Secret Teachings of All Ages,* gives evidence in several places that an esoteric language was taught and spoken in the Temples of the Ancient Mysteries:

> The temples of the ancient Mysteries evolved their own sacred languages, known only to their initiates and never spoken save in

the sanctuary. The illumined priests considered it sacrilege to discuss the sacred truths of the higher worlds or the divine verities of eternal Nature in the same tongue as that used by the vulgar for wrangling and dissension. A sacred science must be couched in a sacred language.

There are some subtle indications given within the esoteric poem *Parzival* by Wolfram von Eschenbach that the legend of the Holy Grail was originally obtained from an 'Arabic writing' that was an interpretation of information written in the 'Stellar Script.' Trevor Ravenscroft, in his esoteric interpretation of this poem, *The Cup of Destiny*,[1] points out that the code word used in the poem to veil the secret of its origin is 'Flegetanis,' which in the ancient Persian language means 'stellar script.' Steiner says that there are many such esoteric works written in this script that are preserved in the 'akashic records.' He also states that all significant cosmic events are recorded in this 'symbolic sign language.' These can be read and even translated, he tells us, by those initiates with both a developed clairvoyant perception and an understanding of the esoteric script. Brother Djwhal Khul, throughout his many books, translates excerpts from a very ancient Sensa writing that he calls the *Old Commentary*.

> These old scriptures are not read in the way modern student read books. They are seen, couched and realized in a flash. Let me illustrate: —The words, ' One enunciates the Word which drowns the triple sound' are depicted by a shaft of light ending in a symbolic word in gold superimposed over three symbols in black, rose and green. Thus are the secrets guarded with care.[2]

According to Steiner, Mabel Collins wrote *Light on the Path* in this way. One night, he tells us, while her body slept, she visited 'the Hall of learning' where she was told to closely observe the patterns and signs that formed along one wall. These signs, she soon discovered,

---

[1] Samuel Weiser, 1982, p. 13
[2] *A Treatise on White Magic*. Pages 75-76.

could be read as an open book. Then after returning to her body she was able to translate the patterns into the book, *Light on the Path.*[1] D.K. tells us that Master Hilarion, who in an earlier incarnation was Paul of Tarsus, was the author of this scripture. H. P. Blavatsky, 'an initiate of high standing,'[2] was another such person. That she could read this 'Mystery Language,' as she called it, using intuition and her developed clairvoyant perception, is demonstrated in the two 'Senzar' works that she translated from the astral light, *The Book of Dzyan* and *The Voice of Silence. The Book of Dzyan* forms the basis for her famous book, *The Secret Doctrine,* which in one sense is a very lengthy commentary upon it. In her *Theosophical Glossary* she defines 'Senzar' as "the mystic name for the secret sacerdotal language or the 'Mystery Speech' of initiated Adepts, all over the world." In her *Secret Doctrine* she writes,

> The seven keys to the Mystery Tongue have always been in the keeping of the highest among the initiated Hierophants of antiquity. It is only the partial use of a few out the seven which passed, through the treason of some early Church Fathers—ex-Initiates of the Temples—into the hands of the new sect of the Nazarenes. Some of the early Popes were Initiates, but the last fragments of their knowledge have now fallen into the power of the Jesuits, who have turned them into a system of sorcery.[3]
>
> We have now to speak of the Mystery language, that of the prehistoric races. It is not a phonetic,[4] but a purely pictorial and symbolical tongue. It is known at present in its fullness to the very few, having become with the masses for more than 5,000 years an absolutely dead language... A few instances may be given. On the plane above, the Number is no Number but a *naught*—a CIRCLE. On the plane below, it becomes *one*—which is an odd number. Each letter of the ancient alphabets having had

---

[1] See Rudolf Steiner's *From the History of the First Section of the Esoteric School 1904-1914*, page 451-452.

[2] See Alice Bailey's *Telepathy and the Etheric Vehicle*, p. 140

[3] *Secret Doctrine*, Adyar Edition, Vol. 2 page 23

[4] While the Mystery language is primarily pictorial it does have a corresponding sound equivalent.

its philosophical meaning and *raison d'être*, the number 1 signified with the Alexandrian Initiates a *body erect*, a living standing man, he being the only animal that has this privilege. And, by adding to the 'I' a head, it was transformed into a P, a symbol of *paternity*, of the creative potency; while R signified a "moving man," one on his way.[1]

'The plane above number' is the unmanifested formless reality (*shunyata*) where no differentiation is possible. 'The plane below' is the manifested universe of number and form, the highest of which is the all-inclusive One. In the preface to her translation of *The Voice of Silence* Blavatsky states:

> The sacerdotal language (Senzar), besides an alphabet of its own, may be rendered in several modes of writing in cipher characters, which partake more of the nature of ideographs than syllables . . . The easiest way [to read them], however, is that which allows the reader to use no special, or any language he likes, as the signs and symbols were, like Arabian numerals or figures common and international property among the initiated mystics and their followers...

Rudolf Steiner has also translated some writings recorded in the Akasha Chronicles in his book on the ancient history of the Earth, *Cosmic Memory*.

> Only with difficulty can the writings in the Akasha Chronicle be translated into our colloquial language. They are more easily communicated in the symbolical sign language used in Mystery Schools, but as yet the communication of this language is not permitted.

The Language of Symbols, says Steiner, transcends the illusion and division of egotistical thinking. This is because the represented

---

[1] S. D. II, 2, XXIV

symbols primarily depict whole systems, principles, and laws, which an egotistical consciousness cannot discern.

> The language of ordinary life was not used in occult schools, but a language that worked upon the human being in quite a different way. For it was a language that worked not by means of words and thoughts as is the case with ordinary knowledge, but by means of *symbols*. Those of you who know mathematics will readily understand why symbols were chosen for this purpose; for symbols have a universal meaning. By developing oneself up to the stage of a language that speaks in symbols, one was able to step beyond the egoism that confuses judgment and clouds ordinary consciousness. This meant however, that what one was able to say was comprehensible only to those who had first learned the language. The language consisted of symbols that could be drawn, or traced with movements of the hand in rituals, or expressed in colour combinations and so forth. In occult schools it was not what was imparted in words that was important, for that was only preparatory, but rather that which was spoken in symbols, independent of ordinary human words, independent even of ordinary human thoughts. Thus, the first step to be taken in an occult school was the study of the symbol language.[1]

Rabbi Simeon states in the *Book of Light* that the *Torah*, the laws of Moses, was originally given, not is Hebrew, but in the 'Holy Tongue.' Rudolf Steiner, in his lectures on Genesis, confirms this. H.P. Blavatsky, in papers left behind after her passing, gives some of the original symbols that were used in the opening lines of the *Book of the Beginning (Genesis)*, from which the modern Hebrew rendering is said to have been taken:

> The head of a bull within a circle, a straight horizontal line, a circle or sphere, then another one with three dots in it, a triangle,

---

[1] From a lecture given June 2, 1912 and recorded later in the book *Man in Light of Occultism.*

then the Swastika (or Jaina cross); after these come an equilateral triangle within a circle, seven small bulls' heads standing in three rows, one over the other; a black round dot (an opening), and then seven lines, meaning Chaos or Water (feminine).[1]

From a collection of early Welsh manuscripts pertaining to the Bardic Mysteries of Great Britain we learn that there are basically three kinds of symbols, those of music, those of numbers, and those pertaining to the Coelbren, the mystic language of creation, which is the most ancient of the three. The 'Bards of the Isle of Britain' considered the Coelbren to be one of their greatest secrets.[2] According to Porphyry (234-305 AD) Pythagoras taught that numbers each had a hieroglyphic symbol, which when taken together explained the nature of all things.

The original Rosicrucian Brotherhood, established by Christian Rosenkreutz in the 14th century, maintains that the esoteric language in their possession was the original language from which all other languages were derived. In their *Confessio Faternitatis* written by Rosenkreutz, we find the following declaration:

> We have a magic writing, copied from that divine alphabet with which God writes His will upon the face of celestial and terrestrial Nature. . . In the same way that God has placed the characters of His alphabet in the holy Scriptures, so has He imprinted them most clearly, during the miracle of His creation, in the heavens, the earth and the animals.... We have derived our magic entirely from such characters and on this foundation have constructed a new language in which the essence of things can be expressed.

In the *Rosicrucian Fama Fraternitatis* or *The Declaration of the Brotherhood,* also by Christian Rosenkreutz, we find this suggestive

---

[1] *The Secret Doctrine,* Adyar Edition, Vol. 5, page 206.

[2] See The Barddas by Rev. Williams Ithel, Llandovery 1862 This work contains a wealth of veiled information on our subject..

statement: "Before our eyes we behold the images and patterns of the whole world." For anyone familiar with the 'images' that flash 'before our eyes' there can be little doubt as to the intended meaning. These images of light geometrically depict the archetypal 'patterns of the whole world.' The mysterious and now lost Rosicrucian *Book M,* which according to the *Fama Fraternitatis* was translated into Latin by Christian Rosenkreutz may have been originally written in this angelic language. J. Van Rijckenborgh, the Rosicrucian initiate, describes this book.

> The pages of the *Book M.* are filled with wonderful letters and singular characters. It is as if they were alive… Your eye is captivated by tremendous waves and the gentle yet mighty heaving of the infinite depths. Yes, the Book M. speaks a magical language. When the locks fall open and the formulas are pronounced, the senses are transcended and one rises above matter, ascending, in the openness of etheric life, to the unseen.[1]

The Rosicrucian *Fama Fraternitatis* also states that Theophrastus (Paracelsus) "though not a member of our Brotherhood had diligently read the Book M." This may have been Rosenkreutz's Latin translation. This book, says the *Fama*, contains "our magical language, with a large dictionary, which we yet use daily to the praise and glory of God and do find great wisdom therein."

John Heyden (1629-1667), a student of the Rosicrucians, in his *Temple of Wisdom*, states:

> According to the Doctrine of Celestial Writing we know of the mutations that shall happen on the Earth because we see that they are written in the Heavens.[2]

In his *Wise Man's Crown* Heyden writes:

---

[1] *The Call of the Brotherhood of the Rosycross: Esoteric Analysis of the Fama Fraternitatis R.C.* by J. Van Rijckenborgh. Page 34.
[2] Page 156.

In the *Temple of Wisdom* you see obscure figures of Astronomy and Geomancy, wherein is added the alphabet of the Angles or writing of the Language of Heaven, affording compendious words partly by stars and characters set in the manner of a wheel... Concerning these secrets my ingenious disciple, if it were lawful to tell you I would.

Robert Fludd, in his *Apology for the Brethren of the Rosy Cross,* rightly states that the letters of the Hebrew alphabet have the power of the sounds of the Language of the Angels but not the form. He also states that the Tablets of the Law, which Moses received from the burning bush of God, were originally written in the Language of the Angels.

Rudolf Steiner, in a lecture given June 6 1904, says that the Rosicrucians taught the 'reading of the esoteric script' as part of their training. This statement is confirmed by an anonymous author of an 'early unpublished Rosicrucian manuscript.' This manuscript, quoted by Manly P. Hall in his *Secret Teachings of all Ages,* states that at the stage or level of Rosicrucian development called 'Mount Quabbalah' the students learns "the language of angelic or celestial beings. He who masters it is able to converse with the Messengers of God." [1] According to Steiner there are seven stages of Rosicrucian development and training:

    1. Study

    2. Imaginative knowledge

    3. Reading of the esoteric script

    4. Preparing the Philosopher's Stone[2]

    5. Understanding the correspondence between the macrocosm and the microcosm

    6. Living in the macrocosm

---

[1] See page CXLIV upper right.

[2] In his book *Rosicrucian Wisdom*, Rudolf Steiner, while not actually revealing the secret of the Philosopher's Stone, gives some illuminating hints as to its nature. The secret of the Philosopher's Stone is discussed in my book *A Synthesis of Alchemy* Pentarba Publications 1994

7. Divine bliss

The third stage relates to the esoteric script. This is not ordinary writing but relates to the secrets of nature…. There are hundreds and thousands of such signs that the student gradually learns. Such signs are not arbitrary, but enable those who understand them to immerse themselves in things and experience their essential nature directly. Study [the first stage] trains the faculty of reason; imagination [the second stage] trains the life of feelings; and knowledge of the esoteric script [the third stage] takes hold of the will. It is the path into the world of creativity. If study brings knowledge, and imagination brings spiritual vision, knowledge of the esoteric script brings magic. It brings direct insight into the laws of nature that lie dormant in things— their very essence…. Such signs used to be considered sacred, at least by initiates. If we go back far enough, we find that strict rules were imposed concerning their secrecy, incurring severe punishment when broken, to ensure they were not used for unworthy purposes.[1] In very ancient times those who were initiated in the Mysteries were under strict injunction not to betray to people outside anything of the Mystery Language; for if a man who was outside the Mysteries were to get to know the symbols and were clever enough, he might come to possess—all unprepared—a means to occult knowledge. The creation of the symbols provided the possibility of a language common to all men. The keeping secret of the symbols prevented the knowledge that was expressed in them from reaching those who were unripe to receive it. Thus, through the very fact that one was obliged to speak and use a symbolic language, provision was at the same time made against Mystery knowledge being communicated indiscriminately. I leave it to the student to discover the hidden meaning, for it is in this self-discovery that the real meaning of the higher worlds, the world of archetypal

---

[1] *The Secret Stream: Christian Rosenkreutz and Rosicrucianism.* By Rudolf Steiner P. 52 & 53

images, will be discovered. Such symbols were in frequent use, and there were earnest assemblies in which the language of symbols could be learnt. I shall say no more about the matter than this, for the schools of Initiation guarded these symbols very strictly, communicating them to nobody who had not pledged himself silent about them. To be a genuine knower a man needs only to have mastered the symbolic language—that is to say, a certain symbolic script.[1]

In the *Qur'an* King Solomon is quoted as saying that he had "been taught the Language of the Birds," which is undoubtedly a veiled reference to the language of angels.[2] Fulcanelli, in his alchemical classic *The Mystery of the Great Cathedrals,* states:[3]

Argot (Cant) is one of the forms derived from the 'Language of the Birds,' parent and origin of all other languages—the one spoken by philosophers and diplomats. It was knowledge of this language, which Jesus revealed to his Apostles, by sending them the spirit, the Holy Ghost. This is the language, which teaches the mystery of things and unveils the most hidden truths. The ancient Incas called it the Court Language, because it was used by diplomats. To them it was the key to the double science, sacred and profane. In the Middle Ages it was called the Gay Science and the Gay Knowledge, the Language of the Gods, the Dive-Bouteille…. Today, apart from Cant, we find its character in a few local dialects, such as Picard, Provencal, etc. and in the language of the Gypsies.[4]

Many of the Gothic churches and cathedrals of Europe were built, says Fulcanelli, using the symbols and proportions as taught in

---

[1] From a lecture given in Dornath the 10th of Oct. 1915.

[2] *Qur'an 27: 16*

[3] *Le Mystere des Cathedrales*

[4] It has been showed that a large part of the language of the Gypsies is derived from Sanskrit.

the Sacred Mysteries. This is also true of many of the temples and stupas of the East.

Dionysius the Areopagite, the father of Esoteric Christianity, wrote a very remarkable series of esoteric books,[1] which according to Rudolf Steiner contain the original oral teachings of the esoteric school established by the Apostle Paul in Athens.[2] His books were at first accepted by the church but was later rejected as 'containing suspicious material not found in the scriptures.' They nevertheless had a profound influence upon the evolution of European thinking in the early centuries of Christianity. They speak of the Mysteries and the secrets of Initiation and even reveals the existence, maybe for the first time openly, of a secret Brotherhood, a "Hierarchy of Initiates and spiritual beings that uphold the living multidimensional structure of the cosmos," and who transmit their wisdom during initiation "through sacred symbols."

> We contemplate the divine Mysteries by way of those symbols that are naturally attached to them. What is necessary is to uncover these symbols, to see them in their purity. By contemplating them in this way we gain not only a reverence for them but we begin to perceive how the ever-flowing source of life arises within itself as a simple and unique power, the wisdom of all wisdom by its own self-contemplation.[3]
>
> The Hierarchy has given to each a name or symbol to signify its essential nature. The sacred symbols are tokens, perceived by the senses, of truths that are perceived only by the mind. The symbols lead one to an understanding of these mental truths because they are the source of the perceived manifestations of Hierarchy.[4]

---

[1] The works of Dionysius the Areopagite include: *Mystical Theology, The Celestial Hierarchy, The Ecclesiastical Hierarchy, and The Divine Names.*

[2] See *Esoteric Christianity* a lecture given by Rudolf Steiner Nov. 27, 1906 and Acts of Paul 17: 34

[3] Letter IX.

[4] *Ecclesiastical Hierarchy.* 2: 3.

Whatever our inspired sacred Initiates set down for us in the holy tablets of written scripture is to be honored. Furthermore, what ever is given by these sacred men in a more immaterial initiation…mind to mind, this too our leaders have revealed through verbal expression and thus corporeal, but also in a more immaterial form that is free from writing. The inspired Hierarchs have transmitted these things not only in common as a part of the sacred act of undisguised conceptions, but also in the sacred symbols. For not everyone is holy and as the scriptures affirm, this knowledge is not for everyone. The highest leaders of our Hierarchy received their fill of the sacred gift from the transcendent Deity. Then divine Goodness sent them to lead others to this same gift. Like gods, they had a burning and generous urge to secure the uplifting and spiritualization of their followers. And so, using images perceived by the senses they spoke of the transcendent. In their written and their unwritten initiations they brought the transcendent down to our level as they had been commanded, not simply because of the profane from whom the symbols were to be kept out of reach, but because, as I have stated, our own Hierarchy is itself a symbol for what we are.[1]

The meaning of the symbols have been revealed to the divine initiates but it is not permitted to explain them to anyone who has not been initiated.[2]

Dionysius the Areopagite states that the divine Light illuminates the meaning of the sacred symbols during what he calls the 'immaterial initiation' (initiation on levels higher the physical). He maintains that his own clairvoyant sight was awakened in this way. The inner vision of the sacred symbols, he says, is attained only through communion with Hierarchy.

---

[1] *Ecclesiastical Hierarchy.*

[2] *Ecclesiastical Hierarchy* 1

From the perspective of Vajrayana Buddhism, the 'enlightened speech' of the Buddha is expressed in secret by the yogis of the Great Perfection (*dzoqchen*) tradition of Tibet and India through what is called the 'symbol language of the Dakinis' (*mkha' 'gro'i brda' skad*), an essence language that is said to accurately express the nature of transconceptual reality. This language, which they consider to be a part of their most secret sciences, is not taught openly. It must be discovered through meditation and the development of clairvoyant vision. According to the Buddhist texts on the subject, which includes the great *Kalachakra Tantra*, it is used by Arhats (adepts) to transmit the highest most secret spiritual truths to their disciples. It is also used by them to communicate with other Arhats of the same or greater understanding.

The creative language of the gods, Devas or Dakinis is made up of thought patters of psychic energy that become clairvoyantly visible to an initiate of a certain degree. Many of the genuine hidden teachings (*termas*) left by the Padmasambhava were either physically written and sealed in this secret script or as symbolic thought-forms in space. Some of the physical termas discovered by Jigme Lingpa (1730 to 1798) were written in this symbolic script. He writes of one such teaching that he discovered:

> As I slowly opened the Teaching I saw a cluster of symbolic Dakini letters inside the outline of an image of a stupa. I could not read them.[1]

Later, he tells us, he was taught to read them by the Dakini Yeshi Sogual, consort of Padmasambhava, who appeared to him at his campsite. He was thus able to develop his consciousness to the degree where "all phenomenal appearances turned into signs and gestures of the Dharma."[2] Jigme Lingpa, who is considered to be one of the greatest of all 'treasure revealers' states that most of the termas or

---

[1] *Secret Words of the Dakinis.*

[2] *Apparitions of the Self.* By Janet Gyatso p. 122

'mind transmissions' said to be from Padmasambhava were not genuine. The script of the Dakinis is seldom written down. It is primarily communicated through mentally sent pictures. (The term 'Sensa' in Latin means 'thought teaching.') Do Khyentse Yeshe Dorje received such a vision as the 'Last Testament' of his teacher, Dodrup Chan Rinpoche, who, he says, appeared to him in his light body at the time of his passing.

> This Testament, which appears clearly in the symbolic script of the Dakinis. May it remain stable. May it be kept secret, closed like a tomb, until the time arrives. This symbolic sign will not disappear.[1]

Lobsang P. Lhalangpa, in his translation of Takpo Tashi Namgyal's monumental treatise, *Mahamudra: the Quintessence of Mind and Meditation* writes of the two levels of the power of Mystic Speech. The highest of the two levels he says is supermundane communication.

> Supermundane communication [is] based upon the symbols of transformation, as in the case of that which happens between meta-cosmic Buddhas and the attending bodhisattvas of the highest order.[2]

Janet Gyatso writes briefly, in her *Apparitions of the Self*, of the close connection that exists between the Dakini language of symbols and the *Samdhabhasa*, the secret language used in the Hindu and Buddhist tantra. According to certain scriptures of ancient India, the Rishis, through the practice of yoga, were able to unite their consciousness with *Paravac*, the supreme WORD. Through this they were able to understand the essential archetypal patterns behind the evolution of consciousness as it is stepped down through the nerve centers (*chakras*) of all living organisms and as it is further differentiated into the petals (cyclic activity) of those chakras, each

---

[1] See *Autobiography of Do Khyentse Yeshe Dorje.* 107 a/4

[2] Page 416

with its own vibration, pictorial geometry and sound. The Rishis, it is said, evolved from this unique awareness a complete esoteric science and language, which they called *Samdhabhasa* (sometimes spelled *samdhyabhashya*). This term is usually translated as 'twilight language.' However, by reducing the Sanskrit term to its essential aspects we may gain some insight as to its esoteric meaning. The prefix '*sam*' means unity, united, inclusive, '*dhya*' means to meditate, to focus the mind, and '*bhashya*' means language. The image that comes to mind is a language where unified ideas are perceived and even communicated through the mind in meditation. John Davidson, in his book *The Web of Life* briefly speaks of this secret 'Language of the Rishis.'

> This idea of what is essentially a natural language encoded into the Akashic level of man's existence, reflecting the patterning of physical life below, and linked into the patterning of his antashkarana [field of consciousness], ready for conscious use, is quite fascinating, for it means that given a higher consciousness, man would possess an instinctive language; that we have not been born into a Tower of Babel, but have only made it so by our lower consciousness. [1]

The images of transcendental wisdom that miraculously appear to the yogi in meditation constitute one of the subjects discussed in the practice (*sadhana*) portion of the six-branched yoga of the great *Kalachakra Tantra*. By stilling the thought producing mechanism and by turning off the senses (*pratyahara*) the yogi enters a deep silence. By remaining in the silence and by focusing the attention at a point between the eyebrows, certain light images called 'empty forms' naturally and spontaneously arise to the inner vision. According to Dolpoba (1292-1361), the great Kalachakra master, these 'empty forms' (*sunya-bimba*) are a direct expression of the Buddha Nature, the spiritual essence within all beings.[2] The great Mahasiddha Naropa says

---

[1] P. 281-282

[2] See *The Buddha from Dolpo*, by Cyrus Stearns, State University of New York Press, 1999, page 99

that while these 'empty forms' are empty of any reality of their own they nevertheless clearly and directly reflect reality.

Hermes Trismegistus may have been referring to the same archetypal forms when he states that when his 'bodily senses had been restrained' the god like being Poimandres unveiled for him the Light from which arose the WORD as a 'Voice of Light.'

> 'Fix your mind upon the light,' said Poimandres. And in my mind I saw that the light consisted of innumerable powers from which arose the ordered world, but without any limits.... 'What you have seen in your mind,' said Poimandres, 'is the Archetypal Form, which is prior to the beginning of things and is without limit."

H. P. Blavatsky states:

> Zen-(d)-zar, the sacerdotal language, is in use among the Initiates of archaic India. Found now is several indecipherable inscriptions, it is still used and studied unto this day in the secret communities of the Eastern Adepts, and called by them — according to locality — Zendzar and Brahma or Deva-Bashya.[1]

Deva-Bashya, sometimes spelled devabhashya, means speech of the *Devas,* angelic like beings of the subtle world. The 'Brahma' or Brahmi script is an ancient Indian language considered by some language experts to be the origin of the present form of the Sanskrit alphabet.

It may seem from all this that each culture has invented its own particular secret language, and to a small degree this may be the case. It is certainly the way most academic historians would interpret the data. But before we come to any conclusions on this it might be wise to consider the international and multicultural nature of the Sacred Mysteries as well as the fact that the fundamental archetypes, upon which each of these occult languages are said to be based, remain the

---

[1] Blavatsky. *The Theosophist.* Oct. 1883. Editorial Note on Zoroastrianism.

same regardless of which culture or religion has discovered them. If we trace the history of the most obvious archetypal symbols, such as the five or six pointed star, the triangle, and the cross, we see that they were used by the esoteric community of nearly all cultures with nearly the same meaning.[1] H. P. Blavatsky, who was the first to establish a world movement based upon the essential unity and common origin of all world religions, worked hard all her life to demonstrate the universality and oneness of the Esoteric Doctrine. In an article written for the La Revue Theosophique, she states that Ammonus Saccas, with the encouragement of Clement of Alexandra "learned the mystery-language by teaching the *common origin* of all religions."[2] From the point of view of the Sacred Mysteries each founder of a world religion perceived the same Divine Archetypes, each from their own perspective, cultural environment, and level of attainment. The seeming contradictions, that usually arose later, even within the same religion, pertain primarily to the dogmatic details that become distorted and fixed over time. Blavatsky states:

> Every theology, from the earliest down to the latest, has sprung, not only from a common source of abstract beliefs, but from the one universal esoteric or 'Mystery' Language.

If the mystery language is truly based upon higher truth and if the essential nature of all world religions is likewise based upon revelations of higher truth, it should not be too difficult to realize that all true and accurate theology will follow the patterns expressed in the archetypal language of the One Life. Blavatsky continues:

> There was a time, when the [mystery] language was known to the Initiates of *every* nation, when the forefathers of the Toltec [the Fifth Race] understood it as easily as the inhabitants of the lost Atlantis [the Fourth Race], who inherited it in their turn from the

---

[1] See the *Migration of Symbols*, by Count Goblet d'Alviella, 1894.
[2] Le Phare De L'inconnu. *La Revue Theosophique*, Vol. 1, 1889

sages of the Third Race, the Manushis, who learnt it directly from the Devas [Angels] of the Second and First Races.[1]

Rudolf Steiner states:

> A certain language and script is learned by those who have been initiated into the Mystery Schools. It is through this language that those with all-inclusive knowledge express their experiences. *All* the initiates of the world can write and speak in this symbolic language.[2]

For the sake of clarity let's examine some of the characteristics of the esoteric language that are held in common by the few written sources and fragments that have come down to us.

1. It originates from the spiritual world.
2. It is the original language from which the other languages of the world are mere distorted reflections.
3. It awakens the consciousness to an understanding of higher truth.
4. It has seven levels of interpretation corresponding to the seven levels of being.
5. It has always been kept secret from those who were not initiates.
6. It was originally taught to initiates by angelic type beings.
7. It was taught in the Mystery Schools.
8. The shapes and sounds of its letters directly reflect its essential nature corresponding to the fundamental principles of nature.
9. Through this creative language the spiritual will is implemented.
10. It connects the earthly sphere with the spiritual world.
11. It is revealed to the initiate during initiation into the Mysteries.

---

[1] *The Secret Doctrine.* Vol. 1, p. 25-26
[2] From a lecture given in Berlin 10 Oct. 1904

12. It is particularly suited for communicating wisdom.
13. It is used to impart, mind to mind, the secrets of initiation.
14. It is used by initiates to communicate with each other.
15. It is used as a subtle form of pictorial speech.
16. It is used to veil the secrets of initiation from the uninitiated.
17. It is a natural language reflecting the laws of nature and evolution.
18. It is used to further the spiritual evolution of the world.
19. It is a symbolic expression of the divine WORD of Creation.
20. It is a language of great creative power.
21. Certain words of power sounded in this language connect the initiate with the higher beings and principles with which they correspond.
22. It is a visual and audible reflection of the divine archetype.
23. It is a universal language known to initiates of all countries.
24. It was not arbitrarily devised but rather visually and accurately corresponds to natural principles.

Rudolf Steiner taught that we are immersed in this 'universal language' between death and rebirth, losing our conscious connection to it as we descend into a physical body.

The languages here on earth are adjusted in every respect to earthly conditions, for these languages are an expression of our earthly thoughts… In pre-earthly existence we have a language that is not exhaled from within, but is rather inhaled as spiritual inspiration. There we live within this WORD of the universe, this universal language, from which all things are made. As we descend to the earth we lose this life within the universal language, acquiring instead the means that serve to express our earthly thoughts.[1]

At a book auction I recently purchased a rare and curious little book entitled *The Mysteries of Isis* by Uniche, N.Y. 1858. On the title page it states: "Translated from the original Mythic Symbols." And although it is veiled in many ways it nevertheless includes some interesting observations pertaining to our subject.

> We cannot comprehend the spirit within us, much less those Great Spirits who create, sustain, and govern not only us, but the whole spiritual and material world. Yet we can use certain given names and symbols to represent them; and by their arrangement and interpretation, obtain not indeed the Truth, whose beauty, brightness, and glory we could not bear but the highest correspondences or images of truth, the mind is capable of receiving. This opens to us a new science, which is properly called Mythematics; for it applies to unseen spiritual existences governing matter, the same as the science of mathematics applies to matter itself and its relations. As the one enables us to ascertain the order, revolutions, magnitude and movement of the material bodies of the heavens, so the other applies in a similar manner to those Great Spirits who create, sustain and govern them; and by whose unerring providence all things in the heavens and on earth are conducted. In this manner is unfolded to us the history of creation, of nature, and of man; the different races of man brought into existence, the incarnation of the spirits they represent, together with the powers and faculties they receive, the society or government they instinctively form, their origin, progress and destiny, all of which is found written in mystic symbols. To arrange, interpret and understand them solves the mysteries of the past and is the perfection of human wisdom; and to live in conformity with the rules they give

[1] From a lecture by Steiner, December 2, 1922 in Dornach. *The Inner Nature of Music and the Experience of Tone.* Anthroposophic Press, (1983) p.31.

affords us the greatest earthly enjoyment and the best preparation for a more elevated existence in the future.... In all the larger or more particular correspondences of this science, all arts, sciences and human professions, together with our figures of arithmetic and diagrams in mathematics, the letters of the alphabet, their form and the order in which they are placed and the words of our language are symbols in Mythematics, capable of being used to produce like edifying and corresponding results.

Sensa, the creative language of the Gods, represents the secret speech of Nature, the divine vibrational pattern and impulse behind the manifestation of the physical world. Plato called this archetypal impulse Eidos (Idea-Form). The Sufis called it '*alam mithali nurani*. St. John, following the ancient Mystery tradition, called it the Logos, the divine Word

The Creative Word

In the same way that thought, existing in the sphere of the mind, is transformed into vocal speech by descending to the larynx, so the divine WORD descending from the Ultimate Sphere manifests itself through lesser and lesser planes of being into the mind and soul of humanity.

Sepher ha Zohar (The Book of Light)

The WORD, the paternal Mind, and that within you that sees and hears are not separate, for their union is life itself.

Hermes Trismegistus

To the literal minded we teach the Gospel in the historic way, preaching Jesus Christ and Him crucified; but for the proficient, fired with a love for divine wisdom, we impart the   WORD.

Origen

In the esoteric scriptures of both the east and west, Fire and Light are symbolic code words meaning subtle energies. The phrase from the Great Invocation, "Let Light descend on Earth," is an invocation of the illuminating subtle energies of the universal mind. The WORD is a symbol for the creative manifestation of subtle energies for the purpose of furthering of the evolution of consciousness and spirit. Exoterically the WORD refers to that great word of power that God used to create the world. "And God spoke the WORD and the worlds came into being...and by it all things were made." To the initiates of the Mysteries it represents Cosmic Thought out-pictured as creative thought-forms that provide the Fiery Impulse behind creation and the spiritual evolution of the world. These creative thought-forms, Plato's *Eidos,* are said to be 'sounded' by the Gods of Creation, by the Hierarchy, and by their co-workers in the field (the physical plane). The term 'sounded' is a symbolic code word meaning creative thought. To 'sound' the sacred word, for example, means to create within oneself the spiritual vibrations of the Way or Tao.

The Sacred Word, the OM, is not a physical sound, though it can express itself as one. The Sacred Word is an exalted soul vibration that can be manifested as an audible or inaudible sound. In this way spiritual energy is grounded upon the mental and physical plane for the benefit of the world.

Master D.K. defines this creative process as "the fire of the divine impulse, permeating all forms and driving those forms to certain action and achievement."[1] Fire, when used in esoteric scriptures, refers to the one all pervading primordial energy-substance from which all things are formed and from which all things receive their life, the Shakti of Hindu literature. As a result of the impulse of the WORD the creative fire descends as evolutionary currents or rays energizing the evolution and illumination of consciousness.

In the Egyptian Mysteries the fiery Impulse descends as cosmic rays from RA, the Spiritual Sun. On one level this pertains to initiation. "And Isis spoke and a sweet draught of immortality streamed forth to Horus."[2]

---

[1] Alice Bailey, *A Treatise on Cosmic Fire,* page 401
[2] From the opening verse of the Hermetic work *The Virgin of the World.* Describes initiation into the greater Mysteries.

Because of the dangers involved in this highly creative materialization process the initiates of the Mysteries were not allowed to reveal to the public the specifics of its laws and principles.[1] That which is given to the public on this subject is veiled in symbols in such a way that only those that have awakened their consciousness will understand the hidden meaning. One of the ways in which this veiling was done was through the creation myths such as found in the *Book of Genesis*. A beautiful example of this can be found in the *Zohar (The Book of Light)*, which is essentially a commentary on the *Torah*, the five books of Moses.

> Time had begun. The great pendulum, whose beat is measured by the passage of the ages, commenced to swing. The time for the manifestation into form had arrived. And there appeared a primary point, a nucleus, a seed from which arose the primary substance whose nature was light without color or form. This light-substance radiated out in all directions. Within this substance of light, as within a cosmic womb, could be seen the archetypes of all created forms, latent, yet vital with creative potential. Through the silent action of the divine will the vital sparks of life radiated forth from the primordial point into the great ethereal ocean of forms and became the Soul of the World, the origin of all terrestrial existence. This secret action, ineffable, indefinable, and unknown, was conceived through the instrumentality of the WORD, which is called the beginning (*Bereshith*), for it was in the beginning with God…. In the same way that thought, existing in the sphere of the

---

[1] A few hints concerning this divine creativeness, however, are veiled in Alice Bailey's *A Treatise on White Magic*.

mind, is transformed into vocal speech by descending to the larynx, so, the divine WORD descending from the Ultimate Sphere manifests itself through lesser and lesser planes of being into the mind and soul of humanity. Each aspect [of this manifestation] works in harmony with the Universal Architect; each is obedient to the law of evolution for the fulfillment of humanity's destiny, which is union with the divine.

In the *Book of Mysteries,* an anonymous highly veiled work included in the *Book of Light,* we find this concerning the 'divine manifestation:'

> Before time the boundless One (*En Soph*), the unborn infinite Being, existed without likeness, incomprehensible and un-knowable. In the production of finite existence the first act was the evolution of the WORD (*Memra*), which was the first point in the descending hierarchy of beings.

Another creation myth arising from the Sacred Mystery Tradition can be found in *The Barddas,* a curious collection of ancient Welsh Bardic writings originally compiled by Llywelyn Sion[1] in 1580. This collection was later discovered and added to, unfortunately without designation, by Iolo Morganwg (1747-1874). It was later published under the auspices of the Welsh Manuscript Society in 1862.[2] It has been translated into English as issued by Weiser Books in 2002. In the highly symbolic manner consistent with all authentic occult writings this work speaks symbolically not only of the creation of the world but also of the mythological language that was used in its creation.

---

[1] Author of *The Life of Taliesin.*

[2] Due to the fact that very few other writing from this highly secret tradition can be found to collaborate its subject matter, plus the pervasive prejudice toward occultism in general it the academic community has gone to great lengths to discount it as an elaborate fraud. However, if we compare its highly symbolic teaching with other writings of the ancient Mystery tradition there can be very little doubt that much of it is quite genuine. It has been reprinted by Weiser Books, 2004.

And God sounded His own Name and from this WORD there arose light and life. From the Sound of His Name there arose a fountain of light, within which was contained the life essence of all beings, human and otherwise. The Menw observed this Fountain as it arose in three pillars of light. The image and sound of the three rays of light that issued forth from the WORD were indivisible with the power of God. From this he understood that speaking, hearing, seeing, living, and being were the same, one united with God and that the seeing of the Image was not different than the hearing of the WORD. From the Sound of the Voice he knew its form and appearance. After creating the Earth God drew down the Archetypal-Form, created by the Voice and the Light, to the Earth. On hearing the three sounds of the Voice the Menw understood the three letters of the WORD, and he knew the image or sign that pertained to each. The Voice that was heard was made manifest into form through the symbol and meaning of each of the three sounds. From the three primary letters [of the WORD] were constructed all the other letters. This is the primary secret of the Bards of the Isle of Britain. From this secret comes the knowledge of all alphabets.

In *A Treatise on Cosmic Fire,* we read:

He [the Logos] uttered the Sound, a threefold Sound, one sound for each of His three systems, and started a ripple on the ocean of space. The Sound grows in volume as time progresses, and when it has reached its full volume, when it is fully completed, it forms one of the notes in the major cosmic chord. Each note has six subtones, which, with the first, make the seven.[1]

In another place D.K. speaks of the WORD thus:

Scientific formulas have reduced the most intricate and abstruse discoveries to a few signs and symbols. The next step is to embody

---

[1] *Page 574.*

these signs and symbols into a word or words, thus imparting to them what is esoterically called 'the power of embodiment.' If I might express it this way, the ancient statement that 'God spoke and the world were made' simply means that God's formula for creation was reduced to a great WORD, which He sounded forth and the inevitable results followed. Something of this process on a tiny human scale will be seen happening in the coming age.[1]

The sacred Word, OM, symbolically represents the first letter of the divine name of the Logos. The 'power of embodiment' arises when the word or chord, the vibration of the intended creation, is correctly sounded upon the mental plane. According to the Vedic Mysteries the worlds are created and maintained through the vibrations (*spanda*) of the WORD (*Vac*) sounded forth through four descending levels of divine speech. James Powel clarifies these four levels of speech in his illuminating book *Mandalas: The Dynamics of Vedic Symbolism*:

> The deepest level of speech is transcendental Silence (*para-vac*). On the basis of this unbounded consciousness the seer is able to see sound as it arises from the silent, luminous and transcendental realm, for it does not arise as sound alone but as light. The second level is termed *pasyanti-vac* 'the seeing speech' It is of a level where sound is luminous. Speech on this level has a 'flash like' character. Here speech, the mantra, is seen with the inner eye. Then the seer, tracing the development of this tender impulse of sound as it emerges onto the third level, mental speech (*madhyama-vac*), is able to formulate a thought spontaneously which will eventually emerge on a verbal level (*vaikhari-vac*) as speech which conveys as accurately as possible, the texture of his inner experience.[2]

---

[1] *Destiny of Nations* pages 130-131

[2] Pp. 75 & 76. For a complete dissertation on the four levels of speech as given in Hindu Tantras see: *Vac: The Concept of the Word in Selected Hindu Tantra*

1. Para-Vac — The supreme WORD, the Sound, the Silence, and the Sound of Silence.

2. Pasyanti-Vac — The WORD manifesting as luminous archetypal Images.

3. Madhyama-Vac — The WORD manifesting as thought-forms.

4. Vaikhari-Vac — The WORD manifesting as the physical universe, but particularly as audible speech and physical gestures.

In the same way that physical speech caries ideas into form through sound, so cosmic speech (*Paravac*) caries evolutionary ideas into manifestation through divine thought expressed as subtle sound (*nada*). From the primordial Silence arises the creative Idea, which by seeking embodiment sets up a corresponding Vibration. This Vibration becomes the 'fiery impulse,' through which the Adepts of the Great Work creates those thought-forms that will embody the archetypal Idea and manifest it into conceptual and physical form.

"Besides the sacred language we have a language of Silence."[1] The difference between the primordial Silence (*Paravac*) and lesser forms of speech is said to be the difference between so-called ultimate truth and relative truth.

> (Truth) can be represented by colors, gestures, symbols, and pictorial forms. Ultimate truth is devoid of colors, gestures, symbols, and pictorial forms.[2]

One of the difficulties in interpreting some of the more elevated terms of the esoteric texts is the fact that they often refer to principles of a level where subject and object have not yet been completely separated. The 'WORD,' as the term is used by the Mystery Tradition of both the east and the west is a good example of this. At its highest level, it is said, the WORD represents as a single Idea, the Speaker, the creative Impulse behind the speaking, the vibration which the speaking produces, the act of creating that vibration, as well as the resulting

---

[1] *Leaves of Morya's Garden* II, p.119.

[2] *Vimalaprabha* (1.3.1), the *Great Commentary* on the *Kalachakra Tantra* (1.1d):

archetypal seed in its potential state. *Paravac* is the Silent Sound (*Avyaktarava*), the root source of all vibration both subtle and dense.

The *Book of Light* states:

> The Three primordial elements of nature are fire, air, and water. They are interchangeable one with the other.[1] It is the same with Thought, Speech, and the WORD. Essentially they are one and the same. Their seeming duality arises from the different aspects in which they are observed and understood.

The creative vibration of the WORD, according to the evolutionary impulse behind it, descends from the inexpressible Silence through lesser and lesser levels of manifestation until eventually it manifests as a mere reflection of itself in the world of form. First the creative WORD descends to the mental plane:

> A certain sound of the Logoic Word, when it reaches the mental plane, causes a vibration in the matter of that plane, arrests its tendency to dissipate, causes it to take spheroidal form, and builds it literally into a body which is held in coherent shape by a mighty deva Entity, the Raja Lord of the mental plane.

In the Vedas this entity is called Agni, a powerful deva who embodies the principle of psychic energy, the Fire of Mind. Esoterically understood 'Sound' pertains to vibrating, (activated) psychic energy. By silently sounding the Aum with purpose, the livingness of heart energy, and the organization and form building qualities of the mind, thought-forms that are in-step with Evolution can be created. This is a service that has the potential for broad application for the common good.

The Om or Aum is not the sacred Word itself but rather the physical plane equivalent or correspondence to it as it manifests from archetypal levels of existence.

---

[1] This is now generally accepted by science.

The AUM is man's endeavor to reproduce on an infinitesimally small scale the cosmic triple sound whereby creation was made possible.[1]

The teaching on the sounding of the Om, such as those given in the Bailey Books, are veiled ways of giving secret teachings, to those with ears to hear, on the application of psychic energy, whether as an invocation (Om) or as the creative application of the power of creative thought. The Aum, the sacred word of India, represents, according to their scriptures, but one syllable of the WORD itself.

In the same way that the breath, because of its correspondence with the movement of the energies of the body, in and out, facilitates the projection of psychic energy, in or out of the etheric body, so the silently sounding of the sacred word can facilitate the creation of the needed point of tension, a focus for the vibrating energies for the purpose of creating effects in line with spiritual purpose.

As we investigate these things we must be careful not to separate the metaphysical and physical worlds into two seemingly apposing camps, theological and scientific. The spiritual science of the future will understand that *all* is energy, from the highest internal psychic energies to the energies and substances of physics and that the only difference is the relative speed and subtlety of its vibrations. The subtler the vibration, the greater the velocity and speed of its particles, the greater its truth, unity, intensity, and power. And though it might at first seem otherwise to some, psychic energy, the creative power of thought, is more powerful in its effects than any physical energy. The subtler the energy the purer and more powerful it is.

The early Christians called the manifestation of the WORD, 'the descent of the Holy Breath,'[2] an idea that originated not with the

---

[1] *Initiation Human and Solar.* Alice Bailey page 151

[2] Concerning the term 'Holy Spirit' the *Oxford Companion to the Bible says:* "There is no distinct term for spirit in the languages of the Bible. The concept was expressed by a metaphorical use of words that mean literally, wind and breath (Hebr. Ruah; Grk. Pneuma). The English word 'spirit' is simply an anglicized form of the Latin word for breath (spiritus)."

Christians but with the Sacred Mysteries. When the descent of the Word reaches the plane of mind (*manas*) it coalesces into the seed patterns, the blueprints, so to speak, for its magical materialization into form. These seed-forms, as a kind of spiritual D.N.A., become visible to the mind's eye of the initiate as geometric images of light (*pasyantivac*). The perception of these geometric seed-symbols is a mental, rather than an astral, form of clairvoyance:

> The seeing of symbols…is a special sort of perception and the capacity to tune in on the Universal Mind upon that layer of its activity that produces the pattern-forms on which all etheric bodies are based.[1]

The first differentiation or crystallization of the creative language of the Gods, in the sphere of the mind, takes place geometrically as a wondrous vision of line, electric color, and light. These archetypal 'pattern-forms,' which in Sanskrit are called pasyantivac or visual-speech, transcend the dualistic concepts of the lower mind. At this level of psychic-energy, the language pattern of its intended materialization and the essence of the idea or principle being expressed are still united. Pasyanti speech, we are told, is the primary means of communication between those yogis whose inner vision has been developed. The receiver perceives the transmitted symbols illuminated by the awakened inner fire in the space between the eyebrows, usually with the eyes closed. The Agni Yoga Teaching refers to this symbolic speech as 'signs in space' and 'hieroglyphs clearly outlined in space.' It must be remembered that veiled writing when given by a genuine Initiate or Adept awakens the intuition in those who are ripe for it while at the same time veiling dangerous truths from those who are not yet ready to deal with them responsibly.

> The Great Teacher would sometimes trace various signs in the sand and then erase them. The disciples were puzzled and asked the Teacher why he did not write these signs on something

[1] *Glamor A World Problem*, page 2

permanent. In response, he drew a line [of symbols] in the air and said: 'This is the permanent law. Nothing can erase this inscription.' Thus the Teacher explained the power of thought. Some used to say that the signs in space were as bright as lightning. The Teacher did not deny the possibility of such radiance. 'The time will come,' he said, 'when people will learn how to transmit their signs to distant places.' The disciples could not understand what he meant by these words…. In our abode we value the ability to speak briefly. Such hieroglyphs are clearly outlined in space.[1]

And from another Agni Yoga book we read:

[2]

The Star of Allahabad pointed out the way. And so we visited Sarnath and Gaya. Everywhere we found the desecration of religion. On the way back under the full moon occurred the memorable saying of Christ. During the night-march the guide lost his way. After seeking I found Christ seated upon a sand mound looking at the sand flooded by moonlight. I said to Him, "We have lost our way. We must await the indication of the stars." "Rossul M., what is a way to us when the whole world is awaiting us?" Then taking His bamboo staff He traced a square round the impression of His foot, saying, "Verily, I say, by human feet." Then making the impression of His palm He also surrounded it with a square, "Verily by human hands." Between the squares He drew the semblance of a pillar surmounted by an arc. He said, "Oh, how Aum shall penetrate into the human

[1] *Supermundane* I # 160
[2] From a painting by Nicholas Roerich

consciousness! Here I have drawn a pistil and above it an arc and have set the foundation in four directions. When, by human hands and human feet, the Temple shall be built wherein will blossom the pistil laid by me, then let the builders pass by My way. Why shall we await the way when it is before us?" Then rising, He effaced with His cane all which He had drawn. "When the Name of the Temple shall be pronounced then shall the inscription emerge. In remembrance of my constellation, the square and nine stars shall glow over the Temple. The sign of the foot and the hand will be inscribed above the Keystone." Thus He Himself spoke on the eve of the New Moon. And the heat of the desert was great.[1]

Through visual symbol-speech very subtle truths can be accurately exchanged even over great distances. One of reasons for the use of this kind of communication is that it can accurately express ideas that words and rational thoughts cannot. It also guards against the message being intercepted, as is often the case with mental telepathy. The currents of psychic energy which accompanies strong thoughts and feelings can be observed by a developed consciousness as forming certain geometrical patterns which shift and change according to the flow of thought.

Perhaps an ellipse is evident instead of a circle, or the circle itself changes diameter, or oscillations may be evinced—thus one may observe the impact of thought, if the thought is strong enough. Much that is inexpressible through words may be supplemented by symbols. In every symbol there will be the element of the inexpressible... One should be very attentive to symbols. As secret hieroglyphs they preserve the essence of the universe.[2]

---

[1] *On Eastern Crossroads* by Josephine Saint-Hilaire, page 35
[2] *AUM* # 395

The projected image of feelings of distress is an agitated one. We can observe their zigzags flickering on the screen [of the mind], whereas rapture and exaltation produce perfect circles.[1]

Pasyanti or visual speech, which is a level higher than the usual mantra formulas, can be used as a means of realizing (experiencing) higher truth. By clearly visualizing an archetypal symbol in meditation the experienced yogi who has thoroughly disciplined the mind can tune into its significance, its essential nature. *Pasyanti* speech also represents a way of utilizing pure thought-creativeness to accelerate the evolution of consciousness.

Traces of great thought-creativeness are registered upon the layers of Akasha. This is an illustration of the creative work of the Great Builders, who fill space with their ideas. By the currents of such powerful thought are born the multitude of forms.[2]

An adept will sometimes use this kind of visual telepathy to communicate with a disciple in the field. Sometimes a single symbol will flash like lightening before the inner vision of the disciple, which when meditated upon will be found to contain a wealth of useful information. Perhaps it will represent the pilgrim's 'orders,' keynote, or a new name that will accurately express his or her status, spiritual family, etc. One of the tests given before a certain initiation lies in the correct interpretation and execution of a command given to the candidate by his or her Master in esoteric script. Rudolf Steiner calls this a 'trial by water.'

The nature of the action [to be performed] is understood by means of the occult script with which he is now familiar. If he recognizes his duty and acts rightly, his trial will be successful. Success can be recognized in the alteration produced by his action in the figures, colors, and tones apprehended by his spiritual eyes

---

1 *Supermundane* 2, 339

2 *Supermundane* I, 108

and ears. Exact indications are given, as the training progresses, showing how these figures appear and are experienced after the action has been performed, and the candidate must know how to produce this change.[1]

The given hieroglyph will sometimes change before one's field of vision revealing thereby indicating an activity or task with a beginning and end. When the task is completed the resulting hieroglyph must match the end result shown in the original. Sometimes a visual 'word of power,' will be seen in motion, such as a rotating cross or a line being drawn. Sometimes parts of the sign will disappear in stages revealing thereby stages of the process. Sometimes the Spirit aspect expresses itself through the pilgrim as a

> SOUND which geometrically forces itself into the vision of the beholder'—a deeply esoteric mode of symbolizing that which cannot be expressed or reduced to the tangibility of form.[2]

H. P. Blavatsky states:

> In one sense, Vach [the WORD] is...the 'mystic secret speech,' which descends upon and enters the Rishis as the 'tongues of fire' are said to have 'sat upon' the apostles.[3]

In the Christian Mysteries the divine WORD is said to descend as the Holy Breath at the time of the baptism by fire (initiation).[4]

> And when the day of Pentecost was fully come, they (the apostles) were all in one place and of one accord. And suddenly there was a sound from heaven as of a mighty rushing wind, which filled the house where they were sitting and there

---

[1] See Steiner's *How to Know the Higher Worlds,* chapter 3.

[2] *A Treatise on Seven Rays Vol..3, Esoteric Astrology.* By Alice Bailey

[3] *The Theosophical Glossary p.* 357

[4] See *Matthew* 3: 11 & *John* 1: 33.

appeared unto them tongues of fire, which descended upon each of them. And they were filled with the Holy Breath.[1]

Plutarch (46-120 AD), a priest of Delphic Oracles, in his somewhat overlooked book, *The Mysteries of Isis and Osiris,* gives a few veiled hints concerning the descent of the WORD during initiation into the Mysteries:

> In the City of Hermes Isis is called the 'Queen of the Muse.' With wisdom and justice She reveals the mystery of the Gods to those who truly carry the sacred symbols [above their foreheads] and who wear the divine vestures [of light]. They carry the sacred WORD in their souls, purified of all superstition and dross. And as in a casket made ready for death, the secrets of the Gods, the shining and clear as well as the shadowy and dark, are revealed according to [the colour and radiance of] their vestures. When the Initiates of Isis, at their death [initiation], are adorned with the vestures [of light] it is a sign that the WORD has entered into them. And with Him [the Hierophant], and none other, they ascend there to the City of Hermes.

Both Rudolf Steiner and H. P. Blavatsky have clearly stated that during initiation into the sacred Mysteries the physical body of the candidate, simulating death, was often placed in a casket for three days while the soul consciousness, in a vesture of light, was guided by the Gods to the place of initiation in the spiritual world. This is undoubtedly the meaning of the Plutarch's phrase, 'as in a casket made ready for death.' St. Paul, St. John, Dionysius the Areopagite, Ibn al Arabi, Hippolyto Joseph de Costa, and Proclus also give hints to the fact that initiation takes place outside the body. According to Master D.K., initiation takes place upon the mental plane. Plutarch's 'City of Hermes,' like Ibn al Arabi's 'Celestial Earth', symbolizes the place of initiation. 'The WORD has entered them,' means that 'they have

---

[1] *Acts* 2:1,4

entered the stream and the stream has entered them.' The 'stream' meaning the evolutionary currents.

The Dionysian Artificers, an extraordinary document on the Greek Mysteries written in 1820 by Hippolyto Joseph de Costa, was rescued from the obscurity by Manly P. Hall who published the work in English translation. Da Costa describes in this work the ceremony of admission into the Eleusinian Mysteries where the candidate stands before three persons representing the sun, moon, and the guardian of the secrets of initiation:

> The Mysteries were not communicated all at once but in gradations in three different parts... These ceremonies, thus far, appear to contain the lesser mysteries, or the first and second sages of the candidate in his progress through the course of his initiations. There was however a third stage, when the candidate, himself, was made symbolically to approach death and then return to life. In this third stage of the ceremony, the candidate was stretched upon a couch, to represent his death.[1]

This 'third initiation' was called the 'gateway to the Greater Mysteries.' The title Initiate is usually reserved for one who has taken the third initiation and thereby entered the Greater Mysteries.

Apuleius, in his *Metamorphosis*, describes in a veiled manner his initiation into the Eleusinian Mysteries:

> I approached the confines of death [initiation] and treading on the threshold of Proserpine [resurrection] and being carried through all the elements, I came back again to my pristine situation [my essential nature]. In the depths of midnight I saw the sun glittering with a splendid light, together with the infernal and supernatural gods. And approaching nearer to those divinities, I paid the tribute of devout adoration.

---

[1] Pages 12 & 13.

The 'midnight sun' is a symbol use in the Mysteries to depict the brilliant light seen during initiation at the end of the long dark tunnel of the physical plane and through which the initiate must enter to complete his initiation. At the third initiation he is confronted with all the beings that inhabit this astral sphere, the infernal as well as the beneficent gods.

Rudolf Steiner, an initiate seer of rare accomplishment, gives us a glimpse concerning the beginning and end of a candidate's initiation into the Mysteries, though concerning the initiation itself his lips are sealed:

> Within the Mysteries in those ancient times every human being who was to receive initiation was led into a special chamber. The walls were black, the whole space was dark and gloomy, empty save for a coffin, or something not unlike a coffin. Beside the coffin those who accompanied the candidate for Initiation broke forth into songs of mourning, songs of death. The candidate was treated like one who is about to die. He was given to understand that when he was now laid in the coffin, he would have to undergo what the human being undergoes in the first three days after death. On the third day there appeared at a certain place, within sight of the one who lay in the coffin, a twig or a branch to represent springing, thriving life. And now the songs of mourning were transferred into hymns of joy and praise. With consciousness transformed, the man arose out of his grave. A new language, a new writing, was communicated to him; it was the language and writing of spiritual Beings. Henceforth he was allowed to see the world—for now indeed he *could* see it—from the standpoint of the Spirit.

In the life of the Buddha there were two events, hidden behind usual mythological veils, which illustrates to some degree the importance that the ancients placed upon celestial music.[1] In the

---

[1] See Bu-ston's *History of Buddhism in India and Tibet.* Translated from the Tibetan by Dr. E. Obermiller, Heidelberg 1032, pages 7-22.

Tushita Heavens, so the story goes, the great Bodhisattva who was destined to become the Buddha, upon hearing the music of the celestial conch, knew it was time to incarnate into a human body for the last time, in order to liberate all living beings from the suffering of birth, illness, old age, and death. After he was married and was living a life of pleasure, luxury, and comfort the celestial Bodhisattvas and Buddhas, who were watching over him, became concerned least he become so attached to his life of pleasure that he would forsake his mission. So, using their powers, they opened his mind to the celestial music so that he might hear and thereby remember his destined path. And so one evening while he sat listening to the music being played by the women of his retinue his mind was opened to the celestial music and he remembered the prayer he made before taking birth: "May I become the refuge, protector, benefactor and friend of all that lives." And thus awakened he heard the words of the celestial Bodhisattvas calling to him:

> "Oh, hero of virtue, remember now thy vow to help all living beings! The hour has come. Depart, oh great Sage, from thy home."

John Davidson, in his landmark book on the Christian Mysteries, *The Gospel of Jesus: In Search of His Original Teachings,* devotes two chapters to the WORD and the Divine Music of God.

> The Divine Music is created by God as His Primal Vibration by means of which He fashions and sustains His creation. External music is heard with the outer ears. The divine Music is heard with the 'ear' of the soul, the hearing faculty of the soul. The soul has two primary internal faculties – the power to hear and the power to see – inner hearing and inner vision. From the vibration of the WORD also issues divine light, self-luminous, soft, nourishing, sustaining, beautiful and bright beyond comparison with the light of this world. Like sound, the light of this world is also a vibration – oscillating electromagnetic energy.

Similarly, within, the soul is able not only to hear the vibration of the WORD but also to see it.[1]

According to Rudolf Steiner initiates of the Mysteries were trained to see, hear, and to experience the divine WORD as the 'primal tone of creation' and the impulse behind the 'evolution of the world.'

> They heard the harmony of the spheres, the seven planets. In the astral world they saw the pictures, in the Devachanic world they heard the tone, and in the highest world they *experienced* the WORD itself. When they raised themselves into upper Devachan they perceived through the music of the spheres how the primordial spirit, Brahma, is divided through evolution into the sevenfold Vach [WORD]. This is the designation of the primal tone of creation that the pupils heard. In it they heard the entire evolution of the world.

The seeing of the image of the WORD, says Davidson, is obtained through the development of the 'eye-center.' Peter Dawkins, in his book *Arcadia: The Egyptian Mysteries*, speaks of this center as:

> The 'eye' of the mind, where the Voice of God can be seen as a thought-form, so that it can be comprehended and a decision made as to how to put the thought into practice.[2]

According to D. K. the two major activities of the ajna center, located between the eyebrows, is "its power to project thought-forms and its capacity to act as an organ of clairvoyance."[3]

For those with a developed intuitive (*bodhi*) awareness the archetypal images of the WORD demonstrate the essential unity of higher truth and divine purpose. Abhinavagupta, in his *The*

---

[1] Pages 289-290.

[2] Page 42

[3] Discipleship in the New Age. Vol. I, p. 112

Paratrisikavivarana, [1] an illuminating work on the metaphysics of language, lists some of the qualities of the WORD manifesting itself through the subtle pictorial language of *pasyanti* speech:

1. This language is not sequential for each image contains within itself a completely unified idea or principle.

2. There is a perfect unity of correspondence between the image and the object it represents.

3. It transcends the duality of mental concepts.

4. It is without thought.

5. It manifests the psychic-energy of the divine will (*Iccha-shakti*).

6. It expresses the higher unity of divine ideas.

The higher the level of the manifestation of the WORD the greater its unity, the less it differentiates between aspects of itself. Rudolf Steiner says:

> It is a peculiar feature of one's ascent into the spiritual worlds that concepts merge into one another, that things to which we refer separately in the physical world become linked and fused together in the higher worlds.[2]

In a series of lectures entitled *Rosicrucianism and Modern Initiation* Steiner tells us that those angelic beings, which we call the Seraphim experience no distinction between subject and object. For them 'subject and object are one and the same.' Buddhism asserts that enlightenment is the realization that subject and object (perceiver and perceived) are essentially the same.

In essence it is simple— one. In manifestation it is complicated— many. D. K writes:

> Advance into the world of spiritual values and into the realm of triadal existence (in which the initiate moves) is definitely an advance into simplicity. It is an advance from the complications

---

1 The Paratrisikavivarana is a lengthy commentary on *The Supreme Three Fold Goddess.* Jaideva Singh has translated it into English as *A Trident of Wisdom,* State University of New York Press, 1988.

2 From a lecture on initiation given in Munich in 1912.

of the multiplication table and its resultant arithmetic into the simplicity of the symbolic formulas of higher mathematics; it is a moving out of the world of kaleidoscopic figures in constant movement, into the world of meaning; it is a process of getting behind the world of effects, realizing that one simple cause or directed movement of energy can set in motion a myriad of effects. This whole theme is one of great complexity and yet at the same time so simple that when the simplicity of the planetary constitution is truly grasped and the analytic disputations of the concrete mind are overcome, the liberated Master enters a world of spiritual endeavor which is free from forms and symbols or the veils which hide the basic truth and the underlying mystery. [1]

Before the Primary Energy of the Divine Idea can fully manifest itself through the creative WORD into physical form its vibration is stepped down from the *pasyanti*-speech of pictorial images to the thought-form building mental sphere of *madhyama*-speech. From the unified pictorial or abstract mind the archetypal seeds, the WORD now enter the womb of the concrete mental world — the conceptual mind. In other words the creative Idea descends from the higher mind to the lower. While pasyanti-speech uses the language of pictorial symbols, madhyama-speech utilizes the language of thought. The creativeness of madhyama-speech lies in its thought-form building capacity. As a means of communication madhyama-speech is mental telepathy.

From the mental plane of madhyama-speech the psychic-energy (*chitta*) of the manifesting WORD descends to the physical plane as *vaikhari*-speech, which expresses the descending currents verbally and through physical gestures. The gesture side of vaikhari-speech finds expression through mudra, eurhythmy, and the spiritual rituals of the Mysteries. Rudolf Steiner gave out some of the basics of eurhythmy, which he says is an application of 'esoteric script' to certain movements of the body. Steiner says that eurhythmy, though still in its infancy, has the potential to be the highest art form. But like all art-

[1] *The Rays and the Initiations*, pages. 149 & 440.

forms it becomes significant and profound only when it is responding naturally to impulses originating from the higher world. The lost art of mudra, fragments of which are still used in both Hinduism and Buddhism, is a gesture expression of the same spiritual language. It is expressed through those hand and body movements that are inspired by and cooperate with the spiritual impulses that arise from the incoming divine currents. In the same way that music inspires movements of the body, so the celestial music when felt by those sensitive to its influence, also compels certain movements of the body. These movements facilitate the flow of spiritual energy being expressed through the body. Most people are familiar with the heart-mudra, where by placing the palms together at the heart center one can more easily channel the in-flow and out-flow of heart energy.

This mudra also represents the 'middle path' and the 'central channel' of ascent between the two extremes, through the fire of the heart. This is represented geometrically by the cross with the heart as the balance point at the center. According to Abhinavagupta the heart is the site of the inseparable union of Shiva and Shakti. [1] The body positions (*Asanas*) of Hatha Yoga and the inspired dance or group ritual movements of the Sufis, Buddhists, Hindus, and Masons are examples of this responsiveness to the spiritual currents. Brother D.K., in his *Letters on Occult Meditation*, writes:

> In the true use of rhythmic movement the effect is to align the three lower vehicles with the causal vehicle, and this lining up— when coupled with intense aspiration and ardent desire—results in a downflow of force from above. This causes a vivification of

---

[1] *The Triadic Heart of Siva*. By Paul Muller-Ortega, page 82.

the three major centres and a definite illumination. When an entire concourse of people is thus animated by a single high desire, when their auras blend and form one united channel for the downflow, the effect is tremendously intensified and can be worldwide in its radius. You have an instance of this in the wonderful Wesak festival,[1] kept so universally in India to this day... This channel is formed by the use of sound and rhythm simultaneously employed. By the chanting of a certain mantram by means of the slow, measured movements that accompany that chanting, the funnel is formed that reaches upwards to the desired locality. The geometrical figures formed in the matter of the plane higher than the physical (which are the result of the geometrical movement of the concourse gathered in that Himalayan centre) form themselves into wonderful avenues of approach to the centre of blessing for the inhabitants, deva or otherwise, from any particular plane. For those who can clairvoyantly view the scene, the beauty of the geometrical forms is unbelievable, and that beauty is enhanced by the radiant auras of the Great Ones Who are gathered there.

When the music of pure thought harmoniously and rhythmically merge with the colors generated by a fiery heart and together weave their way geometrically into the higher realms of truth, viewed clairvoyantly, a new science and a new art from, full of beauty and wonder, will arise.

Initiates, we are told, become aware of the creative speech of the Gods at a certain stage in their spiritual evolution. They begin to hear the Music of the Spheres, see the archetypal images as sacred symbols flash before their inner vision, understand the meaning of the divine ideas and ideals being given by the Brotherhood, the great inner Lodge of the Mysteries, and to understand how these creative evolutionary currents manifest on the physical plane. When the divine images are

---

[1] This festival commemorates the Buddha's birth, enlightenment, and parinirvana (death), all of which are said to have taken plane on the full moon in Vaisaka (May). In India it is often called the Vaisaka Purima festival.

united in the consciousness with their essential meaning it can be said that Sensa, the creative language of the Gods, has revealed itself to the initiate. This facilitates the creation of those thought-forms that are in harmony with spiritual evolution.

Rudolf Steiner tells us that the Rosicrucians at the third level of their training were taught the reading of the esoteric script.

> The third stage is the reading in the occult script, that is, not only seeing isolated pictures but also letting the relationship of these pictures work upon one. This becomes what is called 'occult script.' One begins through the use of the imagination to coordinate the lines of force that stream creatively through the world forming them into definite figures and colour-forms. One learns to discover an inner connection that is expressed in these figures and this acts as a spiritual tone in the harmony of the spheres, for the figures are founded on true cosmic proportions. Our [present day] script is but the last decadent relic of this old occult writing and is molded on it.

It is the lines of force that visually determine the geometric patterns and outlines, a visual view of universal laws and principles. It is the lines of force that outline the pictorial aspects of the SENSA alphabet. Through the higher or abstract mind the practitioner perceives and utilizes these directional lines force to aid the Great Work. The third degree initiate begins to work with these currents creatively through the use of the higher imagination. He 'begins to coordinate the lines of force' into 'definite figures and colour-forms.' When the 'inner connection' or correspondence between these forms and their true archetype in the macrocosm is realized, the keynote or 'tone' he sounds will be in harmony with them.

The geometrical light images of pasyanti-speech have the same relationship to the abstract mind that thoughts do to the concrete conceptual mind, except that for humanity, at least at its present level of growth, the thoughts of the lower mind are produced almost entirely by the personality while the vivid images of the higher pictorial mind descend from the spiritual world, usually unexpectedly, as revelations of light. While astral clairvoyance primarily pertain to the desires and aspirations of huamanity, the higher clairvoyant visions of the pictorial mind, at least in the beginning stages, arises unexpectedly as a descent from above and only when conditions necessary for its manifestation have been patiently developed over time. Plato says, "At the point where the bodily eyes fail in their power to see, the mind's eye begins to perceive distinctly and with exactitude."[1] It is this 'eye of the soul,' says Plato, which perceives the archetypal 'thought-forms' (*Eidos*) of the WORD (*Logos*). It is only through this "organ in the soul," he tells us, "that we can learn the truth."[2] D. K. writes:

> The Kingdom of God is present on Earth today and forever has been, but only a few, relatively speaking, are aware of its signs and manifestations. The world of subtle phenomena (called formless, because unlike the physical phenomena with which we are so familiar) is ever with us and can be seen and contacted and proved as a field for experiment and experience and activity if the mechanism of perception is developed as it surely can be. The sounds and sights of the heavenly world (as the mystics call it) are as clearly perceived by the higher initiates as are the sights and sounds of the physical plane as you contact it in your daily round of duties. The world of energies, with its streams of directed force and its centres of concentrated light is likewise present and the eye of the see-er can see it, just as the eye of the mental clairvoyant can see the geometrical pattern which thoughts assume upon the mental plane, or as the lower psychic can contact the glamours, the illusions and delusions of the astral world.[3]

There are of course several levels and degrees of clairvoyant perception. Etheric vision, which D. K. says is rapidly developing in

[1] *Symposium* 219a

[2] *Republic* 518c

[3] *Telepathy and the Etheric Vehicle* p.53-54

humanity, is an expansion of normal physical vision to include a portion of the subtle usually invisible levels of the physical plane and is perceived, he tells us, through the two eyes. Some people perceive ethereally to a small degree without knowing it. One way to test this ability is to obtain a strong horseshoe magnet and taking it into a completely dark closet look at it with open eyes. If you are patient you may be surprised to see light shooting straight out at each end. Depending upon the degree of development these rays of white magnetic light may be sparkling with colors. Astral clairvoyance perceives the illusive ever-shifting dream world of the collective subconscious, the so-called 'astral plane.' There is also a kind of 'remote viewing' that has captured the attention of some scientists because of its practical verifiable nature. There have even been a few scientific studies done on this with some success.[1]

> Clairvoyance and clairaudience are also possible on mental levels, and we then call it telepathy, and the seeing of symbols, for all visioning of geometrical forms is mental clairvoyance.[2]

"Working with basic geometric concepts," says Rudolf Steiner, "awakens clairvoyant abilities." Some examples of these pure geometric symbols can be found in the unique clairvoyant perceptions of Nancy Lansdale. [3] We will speak more about her remarkable discoveries latter.

---

[1] See Joseph McMoneagle's *Remote Viewing Secrets.* Hampton Roads, 2000

[2] *The Externalization of the Hierarchy* by Alice Bailey p. 8

[3] See *The Archetype Unveiled: A Study of the Sound Patterns Formed by the Creative Word.* By Theodore Heline.

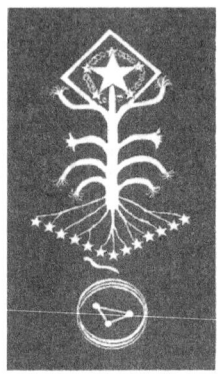 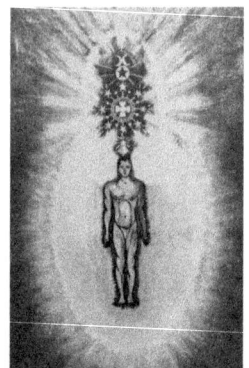

Sometimes a symbolic vision will contain a combination of both natural and geometric symbols as can be seen in this interesting vision recorded by the seer and painter Madge Gladwin

In this visionary painting entitled *The Apex of Humanity*[1] the human constitution is symbolically and geographically depicted. At ground level we have physical plane life. The spiritual path of ascent spirals up the side of the mountain (a symbol that is often used in the Mysteries to represent the mind) to the 'mountaintop experience,'— initiation, illumination, unity of consciousness. The circle of clouds marks the veil that exists between the higher formless (*arupa*) mind above and the rational dualistic conceptual mind (*rupa*) below. From the mountaintop experience a connection is made, which eventually becomes union, with the divine Presence, the spark of the divine within us all.

Paracelsus enforms us:

> Nature emits a light by which we may perceive it from its own radiance. But in man there is also a light besides the light born of nature. This is the light by which man hears, learns, and penetrates into supermundane things.

As the creative vibrations of the WORD are stepped down to the level of mind the spiritual energy is concentrated to a point or fiery-seed (*bindu*), which the yogi perceives as a point of light concentrated in the region of the head (*murdhajoytish*). Many yogis have experienced this light in meditation and have written about it. This light is not to be considered as simply a symbolic or poetic way of speaking. It is a subtle yet brilliant illumination in the head. Vyasa, in his famous commentary to *Patanjali's Yoga Sutra* III, 1, recommends that this light in the head be used as an object for meditation. The great Shankara in his sub-commentary on this verse writes:

> The light in the head is a doorway in the nerve channel in the head. It is radiant and is therefore called a light.

This 'doorway,' which is called *Brahmarandhara*, the 'Hole o Brahma,' is the opening to a subtle passageway through which th

---

[1] From her book *Wisdom is an Ocean*, Johnson 1965, page 168.

prisoner in the body makes his or her escape into the higher worlds. The Kriya Yoga tradition begun by Master Babaji through his disciples Lahiri Mahasay (1828-1898), Sri Yukteswar, and Paramahansa Yogananda teaches that the yogi, at a certain degree of attainment, perceives the sacred word, the OM, as the unchanging light of the soul (*kutasth*), which manifests itself at the ajna center between the eyebrows, like a radiant sun in the head. According to this tradition by unwavering concentration upon this light in the head the yogi can leave the body at will and journey into the higher worlds. According to this tradition the *kutastha* has a dark blue spot at its center. Shankara, in his commentary on the Chandogya Upanishad, also states that the sun in the head is perceive with clairvoyant vision as having an indigo center in which the radiant Solar Beings can be seen. Paramahansa Yogananda, in his commentary on the Bhagavad-Gita, states:

When the Yogi concentrates long enough with half-open eyes at the point between the eyebrows, and when the gaze is without any restless motion, he will be able to see a steady light surrounded by other, but flickering, lights. He should not be diverted by this glimmering halo of the spiritual eye, but should steadfastly look at the center of the eye until he feels his mind completely absorbed within it. In time, he will see the perfect formation of the spiritual eye: a dark opal-blue globe with a quivering ring of flame. Gradually, by deep concentration, an extremely brilliant white [five pointed] star occasionally glimmers in the center of the blue. The star is the gateway through which the consciousness must pass to attain oneness with Spirit.[1]

And D. K., in his *Treatise on White Magic,* writes:

Frequently students speak of a diffused light or glow [in the head]... later they may speak of seeing what appears to be like a sun in the head... Later they become aware of an intensely bright

---

[1] *God Talks with Arjuna: The Bhagavad-Gita: Royal Science of God-Realization.* Self-Realization Fellowship 1995, p. 612

electric light... When this is seen, they frequently become aware of a dark centre within the radiant sun.... This is the entrance to the Path disclosed by the 'shining of the light upon the door.'[1]

He continues by quoting from an ancient symbolic scripture:

Then the Bull of God carries the light in his forehead, and his eye transmits the radiance; His head, with magnetic force, resembles the blazing sun, and from the lotus of the head, the path of light issues. It enters into the Greater Being, producing a living fire. The Bull of God sees the Solar Angel, and knows that Angel to be the light wherein he walks.

When the light in the head (*Murdha-jyotih*), also known as the 'Bull's Eye,' is used as an object of meditation it becomes a spiritual eye through which the yogi sees into the higher worlds. "Meditation upon the light in the head," says Patanjali, "will produce an awareness of that which is subtle, hidden, and remote.... By focusing on the light in the head with one pointed concentration spiritual beings can be seen."[2]

The geometrical light images of *Pasyanti*-speech become visible by fine-tuning the focus of this eye of light. But before this light can appear there must first be an inflow of the Light from above in response to the heart striving of the pilgrim below. John Davidson, in his *The Gospel of Jesus: In Search of His Original Teachings*, states:

When the soul is 'born of the Spirit' – is mystically baptized– and commences the spiritual practice, the first goal is concentration of the attention at the single eye or eye centre. When the attention is active below this point, scattered into the senses, it cannot hear the Sound of the Spirit, the divine Music, which resounds ceaselessly within. Only when some degree of concentration is attained at this centre do the first distant echoes of the Sound become audible... No one can determine, to begin

---

[1] p. 107
[2] Patanjali's *Yoga Sutra* III, 25 & 33.

with, when this sweetest of Sounds will come to him or where it comes from. However, by listening intently to it, deeper concentration is achieved and the soul is gradually drawn up and out of the body, automatically finding its way to the source of the Sound.

Later in the same book Davidson goes on to describe the results that can be obtained by concentrating upon the eye center located in the forehead.

To begin with, the individual experiences nothing but darkness and silence inside. The only 'noise' is the continuous chattering of their own mind. But as the attention withdraws and the mind begins to quite down and concentrate, they begin to experience flashes of light, which slowly stabilizes into a bright and even light. At the same time, the disciple begins to hear echoes of the divine Music of the WORD. Then, by degrees, the soul and mind leave the body and enter the astral realms. Together with these experiences, the mind continually repeating the words or listening to the Sound, a great sense of peace and bliss begins to fill the individual, often continuing throughout the whole day.[1]

Patanjali states that once the mind has been tamed through meditation the unfettered consciousness can then be directed toward the understanding of that which is hidden and to the development of spiritual sight. Rudolf Steiner maintains that our latent spiritual perception can be developed by focusing the light one sees in meditation.

For the student who would develop his capacity for higher seeing, for clairvoyance, it is of great importance to do exercises such as the following. At first, he should picture space as dark, shutting out all light either by the darkness of night or by closing his eyes. Then he should try gradually to penetrate with his own

---

[1] Page 742

inner forces to a perception of light. If he does this exercise in the proper way, the visual perception can be built up as a fully lighted space. Through inner forces the light can be engendered, not a physical light, but a precursor of what later will become visible, not to the physical eyes, but to finer organs of perception. This inner light, in which the creative wisdom appears, is also called the 'astral light.' When the student has awakened this light through meditation, the light will truly become for him the garments of spiritual beings who are actually present, like the Elohim. These Light Beings, such as the human being will one day also become, are even now always present. In this same way all those who have preceded us have come to know the spiritual world, out of their own experiences.[1]

The Agni Yoga Teaching:

In ancient times the initiations into the Mysteries were accompanied by prolonged stays in darkness, until the eye overcame the obstacles of darkness by its inner sight.[2]

The practice portion of the highly esoteric *Kalachakra Tantra* state that clairvoyant perception is developed in the beginning stages in tota darkness. This statement has three levels of meaning, 1) Physica darkness, 2) Pratyahara, or the temporary withdrawal, through yogi control, of the consciousness from all sense perception, 3) and dharan or the stilling the chatter of the conceptual mind. By withdrawing from the sense of physical sight the yogi is better able to see the clear light a the center between the eyebrows. By stilling the conceptual min (thoughts) the yogi is able to perceive with non-conceptual awareness The center between the eyebrows, according to this system, is th entrance to the 'central channel,' which also has three levels of meaning

The light in the head is not to be visualized, we are told, as this can easily create the illusion of light. The true light in the head will

---

1 *Occult Symbols*
2 *Fiery World* Volume 1 No. 316

appear on its own when looked for and when the preliminary practices of purification have been accomplished.

Edwin Babbitt, in his 1878 masterwork *Principles of Light and Color*,[1] also gives a few 'hints' as to how the higher vision might be developed. Like Rudolf Steiner his scientific discoveries were based upon clairvoyant research.

> In the year 1870 I commenced cultivating in a dark room and with closed eyes, my interior vision, and in a few weeks or months was able to see those glories of light and color which no tongue can describe or intellect conceive of, unless they have been seen.... Sometimes fountains of light would pour toward me from luminous centers merging into all the iridescent splendors on their way. Sometimes radiation would flow out from me and become lost to view in the distance. More generally flashing streams of light would move to and fro in straight lines, though sometimes fluidic emanations would sweep around in the curves of a parabola as in a fountain. What was more marvelous than almost anything else was the infinite millions of radiations, emanations and luminous currents which at times I would see streaming from and into and through all things, and filling all the surrounding space with coruscations and lightning activities.[2]

Both Babbitt and Rudolf Steiner state that clairvoyant vision arises from forces acting upon the body from the etheric. In the tenth chapter under the heading, '*How to Develop this Finer Vision*,' Babbitt writes:

> These finer ethers are so swift, penetrating and powerful that it is a very great achievement to be able to wield them for the sake of the wonderful powers of vision, which they give, as well as for

---

[1] I recommend this somewhat neglected work to anyone interested in a scientific approach to psychic energy and the hidden forces of nature. After 150 years it is still ahead of its time scientifically. Unfortunately the common reprint edition is highly abridged. The editor has reduced first five chapters to seventeen pages. He felt the need to remove, he says, all that he thinks is untrue. Only the complete 550-page original edition is of any real value.

[2] Pages 446 & 447.

the great control of both bodily and mental forces that can be gained thereby. I will give some brief hints for the culture and control of these agencies. When convenient it is quite desirable to have a person who is already well charged with these fine forces and who can himself see clairvoyantly, make passes over the head downward and especially over the eyes and forehead, and thus impart his own power to the subject. Sometimes the passes can be made from head to the feet along the face and body, and sometimes one or two inches from the body.... One of the most practical method of developing these forces is to sit somewhat reclining in an easy position with the back to the north or a little north-east [true north?], have merely a dim light rather than otherwise, close the eyes, turn the eye-balls a little upward, if they can be held so without pain, and then steadily and gently make an effort as if to see. This can be practiced for a half hour to and hour or so each time, and while doing so the thoughts should not be allowed to wander, but the aim should be to see if lights, colors, forms, and motion make their appearance. If colors do not appear in a few days, the prospect for clairvoyance is poor unless persons already developed can impart assistance.

The fact that he gives only "brief hints' indicates his caution in revealing of the esoteric secrets concerning the use of psychic energy. According to Steiner spiritual vision can be developed by penetrating into the nature of archetypal images:

Just as the eyes were formed out of the elemental world, the nerves out of the world of spirit, the brain out of the world of reason, the higher spiritual organs are formed and shaped out of the world of archetypal images... Through the patient and vigorous practice of immersing oneself in symbolic mental pictures, we can cultivate these spiritual sense organs.[1]

---

[1] *The Secret Stream*, p. 122

By learning to read the characters of the occult script, we begin to transcend ourselves and delve into the hidden foundations of nature.[1]

All the great seers agree, clairvoyant vision arises only in a refined and purified consciousness that has tamed, to a some extent, the unruly activity of the mind and emotions. Self-mastery is the only way, even for those following the left hand path. Psychism (channeling) is not clairvoyance, but rather the reception of thoughts usually from unknown discarnate beings of the astral plane. At best it is second hand information that is not easily verifiable. "Do not believe anything," said the Buddha, "until it can be verified within your own consciousness." The Age of Aquarius is destined to be a time where belief is replaced with direct knowing.

As we have stated, many of the symbols used in the Mysteries originated from the archetypal images of the higher worlds. When made public these symbols are often either simplified or veiled by depicting them as natural forms, often chosen for their resemblance in some way to the original, either in shape or suggestive meaning. For example, from the perspective of the etheric body the halo of saints, the monarch's crown and the Holy Grail, all symbolize the same archetypal image. When the 'crown' center becomes active, particularly that aspect of it that corresponds to the heart center,[2] the clairvoyant observers perceive the radiation of its energy as a diadem of radiant light around and above the top of the head, so that it sometimes resembles the rim of a chalice or golden crown. Many legends have hinted at this secret. In the *Bible* and as well as in the opening pages of the *Book of Light* it is called the 'cup of salvation.' The Agni Yoga Teaching has called it a 'luminous diadem and rainbow.' Artists of the both the east and the west have depicted their saints with these radiations.

---

[1] *The Secret Stream*, p. 70.

[2] Brahmarandhara.

The descending spiritual fire is visually perceived by the seer as a point of intense light within the circle of its radiance. This 'point of tension,' becomes audible as the sound of the sacred word *(pranava)*. As we shall attempt to demonstrate, the sacred word is represented symbolically by a circle with a point at its center.

A symbol is an outer and visible sign of an inner and spiritual reality, carried out into expression upon the physical plane by the force of the inner embodied life. An emblem is man's formulation of a concept, created by man and embodying for him the truth as he sees it and understands it.[1]

True symbolic signatures can be depicted using either natural objects or geometric forms, often in combination. D.K gives a few of the more obvious meanings for non-geometric symbols:

Air- the buddhic plane (intuition).
Fire—the mental plane.
Water—emotion
Earth—physical.

---

[1] *Destiny of Nations* page 119

A sword—the first ray.
A pen—the second ray.
A golden band of light—the Path.
Door—entrance to the spiritual world.
Sun—the spiritual source.

Proclus, in his *Commentary to Book 1 of Euclid's Elements,* says that while geometry can be expressed in the world of the senses it's true nature demonstrates metaphysical truths. Geometry, he says, allows us to approach universal principles intuitively through images that correspond to them. Students of the Mysteries are exposed to the esoteric symbols early in their training, but the meaning often comes much later as the intuition is developed. The student is taught, not so much the meaning itself, as the means to attain a realization of the meaning directly. To contemplate the true meaning of symbols awakens the intuition. Many examples demonstrating the geometry of spiritual perception could be given. Rudolf Steiner says that many of the symbols of the Rosicrucians originated in this way.

> Among such symbols are the cross, the sign of life; the pentagram or five-pointed star, the sign of the Sound or WORD; the hexagram or six-pointed star (two interlaced triangles) the sign of the macrocosm reflected in the microcosm, and so forth. At the second stage of clairvoyance, these signs - which we today delineate in abstract lines - appear full of colour, life and radiance on a background of light…. The initiates translated their visions into such signs and symbols. The most ancient characters employed in Sanskrit, Egyptian, Greek and Runic scripts - every letter of which has ideographic meaning - were the expressions of heavenly ciphers.

Master D. K., Rudolf Steiner, Paramahansa Yogananda and the 11th century master yogi Gorakhanath, four very reliable sources, have all stated that yogis sometimes see a pentagram within the 'light in the head' during meditation. This vision of the 'Flaming Star,' as it is called in Masonry, blazes forth during initiation into the Mysteries as a direct manifestation energetically of the WORD. In the Masonic mysteries the blazing forth of the star during initiation indicates a direct connection with the home Lodge of the Mysteries, the star Sirius. According to Albert Pike, the great Masonic scholar, the Blazing Star represents the Star Sirius.

Hermes Trismegistus, grand Hierophant of the Egyptian and Greek Mysteries, writes of a vision he had concerning the manifestation of the WORD. In a state of high exaltation and after having restrained the senses the god Poemandres appeared to him and said:

> "The WORD, the Paternal Mind, and that within you that sees and hears are not separate, for their union is life itself. Perceive and understand this as the light within you." As he said this he looked me in the eyes for a long time. And there appeared in my mind a bright light, the intensity of which was beyond description, beyond anything of the material universe. "What you are seeing in your mind," he said, "is the archetypal-form, which is of the original principle that was before the beginning and will continue without end." [1]

Rudolf Steiner states:

> In the Christian Mysteries it was taught that every object first exists as a thought concealed within a being, a thought that is spoken and thus solidified… Everything we see (so said the early Christians) is the divine WORD that has become solid.[2]

According to the ancient Mystery Tradition cosmic forces descending from the heavens direct the growth and evolution of consciousness on this sphere. These evolutionary currents or ray contain the seeds or blueprints of our future growth. To better understand the evolution of the consciousness, therefore, students of

---

[1] *The Poemandres, the Shepherd of Men. Corpus Hermeticum,* 1.

[2] *The Secret Stream: Christian Rosenkreutz and Rosicrucianism* p. 62

the Mysteries study the cyclic appearance of these astrological currents. Most of the great spiritual festivals of the world were originally given to the public by initiates of the Mysteries to mark those points of the yearly cycle when the influences of these streams of energy were at their peak. These festivals also marked certain great spiritual events of the past that pertained to and was the result of these great incoming spiritual energies. These events were kept alive in the mind of the public through stories and Mystery Plays that over time became the allegorical myths that veiled, and also revealed to 'those with eyes to see,' the destined activity of Gods and men. While history records external events, most world-class myths symbolically record portions of an inner spiritual history. One of the striking features of the descending evolutionary currents, as they cycle in and out of influence, is the fact that, though great in the tension thus created at any point in time, they nevertheless maintain a constant harmony in their complicated ever-changing relationships. The Pythagorean philosophers called this relationship the 'harmony of the spheres.' Plato called it the 'eternal pattern:'

> First, we must distinguish between that which is and is never becomes, and that which is always becoming and never is. All that is becoming is the work of a cause. If the manifestation arises from the eternal pattern it is beautiful. If it arises from a created pattern it is not.[1]

By learning this 'language of the luminaries' we can begin to understand the geometric relationships that exists between the heavenly spheres at any given time. It is from these ever changing geometric relationships that the 'stellar script' and the 'eternal patterns' can be read. Traditionally Hermes is regarded as the father of the written language. According to Rudolf Steiner the original Hermes or Thoth was one the first to use the esoteric or stellar script that later became the foundation for all written languages.

---

[1] *Dialogues on Nature*

We must regard Hermes, the great Wise One, who according to Egyptian tradition lived upon the Earth in the dawn of antiquity and was endowed with the most profound clairvoyant insight concerning man's relation to the Universe, as having possessed in high degree the power of understanding and explaining the true nature of the connections between the constellations and the forces of the spiritual world; and of interpreting the signs portraying events and happenings, as expressed in the language of the stars, in terms of their mysterious interrelations. Now, if in those olden days it was desired to enlighten the people with regard to the nature of the bond existing between Osiris and Isis, this matter was put forward in the form of an exoteric legend; but in the case of the Initiates the subject was treated more explicitly by means of symbolical reference to the light which emanates from the Sun and is reflected by the Moon, and the remarkable conditions governing its changes during the varying phases of the latter. In these phenomena the Egyptians found a practical and genuine analogy, expressive of the sacred link between the Isis-Force within the human soul and that supreme spiritual figure, Osiris. From the movements of the heavenly bodies and the nature of their interrelations there originated what must be regarded as the very earliest form of written characters. Little as this fact is as yet recognized, we would nevertheless draw attention to the following statement: If we consider the consonants of the alphabet, we note that they imitate the signs of the Zodiac in their comparative repose, while the vowels and consonants are connected in a way which may be likened to that relation which the planets and the forces which move them bear to the constellations of the Zodiac as a whole. Hence it would appear that in the beginning written characters were brought down to earth from the vault of heaven….It was Hermes, 'The Thrice-Blessed,' who first gave this Stellar Script to the world.[1]

D. K. gives this prophecy:

When the esoteric side of astrology and of mystical geometry has been studied, and alliance has been made between these two sciences, a flood of light will be thrown upon this matter of the intelligent principle…[2]

Astrology might be defined as a study of the evolutionary currents streaming into and influencing our sphere from the Gods whose bodies are the stars and planets. From this it should not be too difficult to imagine that the astrological charts of the future might depict these impulses, patterns, and lines of force in terms of geometry.

Central to the teachings of the Sacred Mysteries is the truth that the seven planetary Gods, externally represented by the seven sacred planets, are in fact the archetypes of the seven primary principles that govern the evolution of the world. Steiner traces this idea back to the temples of ancient Atlantis where each of the seven Gods had its own temple. The origin of the seven toned scale is said to have arisen from the natural correspondences that exists between sound, the seven gods and the seven primordial principles. D.K. hints that the music of future will be composed by translating the harmonies of natural cyclic activity, whether physical and metaphysical, into earthly tones, forms, colors, and rhythms. Iamblichus in his monumental *Life of Pythagoras* states that Pythagoras had not only realized the emotional causes of

---

[1] From a lecture give February 16th 1911 called *Hermes*.
[2] *A Treatise on Cosmic Fire* p. 396

many diseases, an idea that modern physicians are only now beginning to consider, but he could cure these emotional disturbances through a combination of musical cords or voice, by affirming the appropriate rule of virtue, and by displaying certain corresponding symbols. Due to his highly developed sense of inner hearing, says Iamblichus, "He could hear and understand the celestial sounds coming from the central spring and root of Nature."

Johann Sebastian Bach in his *Six Solos for Unaccompanied Violin* cryptically encoded 'in the symbolism of the numerical patterns' some of the musical keys to the mystery of harmonics in relation to the Christian Trinity. The Hilliard Ensemble gives a very beautiful demonstration of this in their music CD *Morimur*.[1]

If we could discover the correspondences that exist between the harmonics of music and natural ecology great strides toward the synthesis of science and art might be achieved. But for this we must first gain an understanding of the inner laws of harmonics. Why is it that certain combinations of notes are considered to be in harmony and can even produce elevating feelings in a refined consciousness, while other, more dissonant combinations, tend to invoke coarse even unpleasant feeling. Many thinkers over the centuries have attempted to tackle this question and yet to this day it remains for the most part unanswered. To understand the true nature of harmonics we must first elevate the consciousness to a point where it can perceive the difference between what is natural and what is unnatural. Proclus, the esoteric interpreter of Plato's writings, defines the term 'natural' as: "That which appears in both the spiritual world and the material world, as a manifestation of the original of divine Intelligence." As we have stated the material world is a reflected image of the mental world, manifesting into form by the creator Gods who pour forth a likeness of the divine paradigm, or archetype, to the lesser gods of the elements. Nature, therefore, is a direct manifestation in the world of

---

[1] In the accompanying booklet to the CD Professor Helga Thoene, who discovered the musical cryptograms, writes a short article called *The Secret Language—Hidden Chorale Quotations in J.S. Bach's 'Sei Solo a Violino.'*

the senses of a divine principle. Part of the problem we have in even approaching this question is our extreme materialistic view of everything. The science of harmonics, like all true sciences, must be firmly based upon a sound metaphysical foundation before it can lead to higher truth. Without this higher perspective, without the enlightened awareness that all things in the material universe are but effects that arises from non-physical causes we will not be able solve the problem. Recently a well-known symphony conductor admitted to some of his colleagues that he was not at all sure anymore what the difference was between music and noise. This confusion exists in the visual arts as well. I once asked the owner of an art gallery if he believed in beauty and he answered by quoting Picasso, "Beauty? What's that?" According to the Hermetic and Pythagorean Tradition, of which Plato and all the great Neo-Platonic philosophers were a part, beauty, harmony, and all that is natural is aligned with the will of the Gods, in other words in step with the current of evolution. The music of J.S. Bach, for example, is uplifting to a refined consciousness because it corresponds, to some degree, with the natural way of things. True art is beautiful for it is reflecting the natural flow of spiritual evolution.

The 'harmony of the spheres' manifests its celestial ecology through the great Law of Equilibrium, which the Sufis called *'Ilm al-Mizan*. The science of harmonics, regardless of the level upon which we may wish to apply it, examines the creation of a unity of interdependent vibrations that change in relation to each other and to the keynote of the whole in such a way that harmony rather than chaos, music rather than noise, is the result. Of course when applied to painting, sculpture, and architecture the harmonic relationships do not change over time except in the moving eye of the observer. The Renaissance architects considered architecture to be 'frozen music.'

The importance of beauty in art and music as a stimulus to the evolution of the human spirit should be obvious to everyone. Unfortunately this idea goes against the dogmatic beliefs of present day materialistic thinking, particularly as taught in the academic community.

There is an ancient prophecy that states that in the coming epoch the esoteric keys to the mysteries of music will be applied is such a way as to accelerate the evolution of the human consciousness. Joscelyn Godwin's important compilation, *The Harmony of the Spheres*, *A Source book of the Pythagorean Tradition in Music*, may contain some of the keys for this.[1] When it is discovered that each note has its own naturally corresponding color and geometrical pattern, and that the changing relationships between notes also produce corresponding rhythmic geometrically changing patterns of color and light, then the harmonious union of music and the visual arts will become possible. From this may arise a direct and accurate artistic expression of archetypal principles and by extension a greater alignment between the higher and lower aspects of the creative mind, the archetypal and rational.

According to teachings attributed to Hermes Trismegistus there are two levels of mind, the 'archetypal mind' and the lower 'formative mind,' or that which interprets ideas according to form.[2] Vajrayana Buddhism also divides the mind into two aspects, arupa and rupa, formless and form, conceptual and primordial. Brother D.K. divides the mind into the lower 'concrete mind' and higher 'abstract mind.'

> The concrete mind is the form-building faculty. Thoughts are things. The abstract mind is the pattern-building faculty, or the mind that works with the blue prints upon which the forms are modeled.[3]

Rudolf Steiner, in a lecture on the *'Four Spheres of the Higher World*,'[4] calls the sphere of the higher mind 'the world of archetypal images' and the lower mind, 'the world of reason.' One of the primary

---

[1] Inner Traditions, 1993

[2] *The Divine Poimandres.*

[3] *A Treatise on White Magic*, p. 365

[4] March 28, 1910

differences between these two aspects of *manas* or mind is that the formative conceptual mind perceives and creates through thought and the higher mind is more visual, it perceives and creates through images. And while there are higher levels of perception than manas or mind it can nevertheless, as Proclus rightly observes, "accurately trace the whole course of evolution from the manifestation of the One into many and the reuniting of the many into One." Only when the archetypal and rational minds have been united to some degree will the science of esoteric signs and symbols be understood. "Such esoteric signs" says Rudolf Steiner, "enable those who understand them to immerse themselves in the essence of things and to experience their essential nature directly."[1] To perceive the essential nature of things the consciousness must first perceive beyond the level of the conceptual mind. D. K., in his *Treatise on White Magic*, observes:

> He has to learn to get [in] back of the thought processes and form building propensities and [there] discover the ideas that underlie the divine thought-form, the world process. He must learn to subordinate his own thought-form building to these ideas. He has to learn to penetrate into the world of these divine ideas and to study the *'pattern of things in the Heavens'* as it is called in the Bible. He must begin to work with the blueprints upon which all that is, is modeled and molded. He becomes then a student-symbolist, and from being an idolater he becomes a divine idealist.[2]

Proclus says that the essence of geometry belongs to the middle ground between the unchanging One, or Monad, on one hand and the ever-changing objects of the senses on the other. The Pythagoreans, he says, classify the essential nature of geometry with the *Eidos,* the original archetypal idea-forms.[3]

---

[1] From a lecture, *Who are the Rosicrucians?* Given March 14, 1907

[2] *A Treatise on White Magic* by Alice Bailey, p. 365-366

[3] See *A Commentary on the First Book of Euclid's Elements* by Proclus, translated by Glenn R. Morrow, Princeton University Press, 1970, page 31

In my opinion the intelligent characteristics of the soul are able to perceive the divine *eidos*, the differences that exist between them, as well as the summit, the flower as they say, of divine Intelligence (*Nous*) itself, which includes the unity of all beings and through this unity perceive the essential unity of life itself.[1]

Plato taught that not only do all natural things have a divine *eidos* (archetypal thought-form) behind them, but that all natural laws and principles do as well.[2]

The archetypal WORD, say the initiates, manifests itself on the physical plane through the power of thought, speech, and word.

Through speech a thought is evoked and becomes present; it is brought out of abstraction and out of a nebulous condition and materialized upon the physical plane, producing (could we but see it) something very definite on etheric levels. Objective manifestation is produced, for 'things are that which the word makes them in naming them.' Speech is literally a great magical force, and the adepts or white magicians, through knowledge of the forces and power of silence and of speech, can produce affects upon the physical plane. As we well know, there is a branch of magical work which consists in the utilization of this knowledge in the form of Words of Power and of those mantrams and formulae which set in motion the hidden energies of nature and call the devas to their work. Speech is one of the keys that open the doors of communication between men and subtler beings. It gives the clue to the discovery of those entities who are contacted on the other side of the veil. But only he who has learned to keep silent, and has arrived at the knowledge of the times to speak can pass this veil and make certain esoteric contacts. Magic consists, we are told in the *Secret Doctrine,* in addressing the Gods in Their own language; therefore, the

---

[1] *The Theosophy of Plato* Book 1, chapter 3.

[2] *Parmedides* Book 3

speech of average man cannot reach Them. Therefore, those who seek to learn the occult language, those who yearn to become aware of the words which will penetrate to the ears of those who stand on the other side, and those who seek to utilize the formulae and phrases which will give them power over the Builders, have to unlearn their previous use of words and to refrain from ordinary methods of talking. Then *the new language* will be theirs and the new expressions, words, mantrams and formulas will be entrusted to their care. The laws of speech are the laws of matter and students can apply the laws governing physical plane substance to their use of words, for it concerns the manipulation of matter on other levels. Speech is the great medium whereby we make apparent the nature of the little system we are constructing—that system of which each human unit is the central sun, for under the Law of Attraction he draws to himself that which he needs. [1]

Rudolf Steiner has this to say on the esoteric nature of words.

If you consider this question with spiritual understanding you will discover that there are particular words, combinations of words and word formulas that have a much greater effect than the words used in every day language. Such word formulas were handed down in the Mysteries. Now you can understand how it is that these secrets were not to be divulged, because by knowing the formulas a person was thereby entrusted with mighty power over his fellow human beings. [2]

Words of power were and still are used by the Hierophant during initiation to quicken the spirit to higher understanding and power. In the Egyptian Mysteries the Hierophant or Initiator was called Thoth, Hermes by the Greeks. G. R. S. Mead, a direct disciple of H. P. Blavatsky and the author of that stupendous three-volume work, *Thrice*

---

[1] *A Treatise on Cosmic Fire*, pages 981-982

[2] Nov. 26,1916

Greatest Hermes, partially veils an important truth concerning this question:

> It is Thoth who taught these words-of-power and how to utter them. He was the Master of what the Hindus would call *mantra-vidya*, or the science of invocation or sacred chanting. These *mantrah* were held in ancient Egypt, as they were and are today in India, and elsewhere among knowers of such matters, to be of special efficacy in affecting the 'bodies' and conditions of that fluid nature [etheric] which exists midway between the comparative solidity of normal physical nature and the fixed nature of the mind. These 'words' were connected with the vital 'breath' and the knowing use of it. That is to say they were only really efficacious when the spoken words of physical sound corresponded naturally in their vowels and consonants…with the permutations and combinations of the inner elements of Nature. They then and only then were *maa* or true or authentic or real— that is to say, they were 'words-of-power' in that they compelled matter to shape itself according to true cosmic notions.[1]

The archetypal images of the abstract mind unify spiritual concepts into holistic patterns. The abstract mind produces what Rudolf Steiner calls 'imaginative thinking.'[2] Ibn' Arabi speaks of this as the 'creative imagination.'[3] This imaginative perception, we are told, is what sees the creative Idea behind the world of conceptual and material forms. And while this awareness is necessary for a higher understanding of physical and conceptual world there are higher levels of perception. Pure intuitive awareness, for example, perceives that even the archetypal idea-forms (*eidos*) behind all material phenomena are but reflections of an endless, boundless, and undivided reality.

---

[1] Vol. 1, 45

[2] See his *The Secret Stream* edited by Christopher Bamford, page 49-52.

[3] See Henry Corbin's *Creative Imagination is the Sufism of Ibn 'Arabi* Princeton University Press 1969

By concentrating upon the archetypal images of the higher mind the yogi can unite his consciousness with the divine principles that they represent. Rudolf Steiner explains:

> When the yogi learns to unite himself with the Archetypes he ascends to the eternal world of spirit. He hovers above the transitory. In this condition it is said that he rests between the wings of the Great Bird, the Swan, the OM. The OM is the way of return—from the images to the Archetype Itself—the ascent into the eternal.

∴

Mind and the Geometry of Sound

Energy has mass.   Albert Einstein

Energy has shape.   Buckminster Fuller

All things in manifestation receive there shape from the ordering One, through mind and number.
Plato

All things originate with mind.   Gautama Buddha

The physical plane is a complete reflection of the mental.   Master D. K.

To put the conclusion crudely, the stuff of the world is mind-stuff.   Physicist, A. S. Eddington

> The realities of the mind are reflected as geometrical images.
> Proclus

According to the most ancient Esoteric Tradition as revealed to us by Master D.K., 'all that exists is based upon sound, or the Word.'[1] Sounds are bursts of oscillating vibrations (energy). A 'word' is a set grouping of sounds (energies) that have meaning only as a group. The creative Word or Sound is a Vibration that has been impregnated with life, meaning, direction and purpose. Creative sounds are the vibrations of very subtle energies produced by the mind. Physical sounds, in fact every thing physical, has a higher counterpart on the plane of mind. Physical sound has creative potency only when sounded on the plane of mind.

This is also true for seed-syllables or *bijas,* which are words of power that relate to, or corresponds with, fundamental principles. According to the Buddhist Tantra, a series of teachings said to have been given by the Buddha after his passing, the seed-sounds for the three divine principles—three aspects of the one primordial Fire—are OM, AH, HUM—pure spiritual energy (Om), heart-wisdom energy (Hum), and the creative energy of the mind (Ah). The physical sounds of these bijas, and all essential sound patterns, correspond to very subtle energies so that when sounded, either audibly or silently, with their higher correspondences in mind, spiritual energies can be invoked and manifested into form.

The manifestation of spiritual energies into the material world is the one of the primary missions that humanity is destined to accomplish. But for human beings to fulfill this exalted mission he must first gain some understanding of what these spiritual energies are. For example, buy sounding the *bija* Hum on the plane of mind, with the refined feeling nature tuned to the sublime nature of heart energy we can invoke that energy. The famous Buddhist mantra *Om Mani Padme Hum,* invokes spiritual energy (*Om*) condensed as the jewel (*Mani),* in the lotus (*Padme)* of

---

[1] See H. P. Blavatsky's *The Secret Doctrine,* page ? and Alice Bailey's *Letters on Occult Meditation,* page 50.

the heart (*Hum*). H. P. Blavatsky, in her *Instructions to the Esoteric Section of the Theosophical Society*, gave the geometrical equivalent for this mantra.

Sensa, a language based upon the natural seed-patterns of living Nature, can be sounded as both audio sounds or pictorial images.

A few years ago a group of scientists, while experimenting with sound and its effect on the activity of nature, discovered that when a certain high-pitched note was sounded, a note beyond the range of human hearing, beavers within the vicinity would immediately stop everything and begin building a dam. This discovery supports the esoteric teachings that maintain that the inner activities of nature are directed, coordinated, and maintained by subtle sound vibrations. Another scientific discovery that gives credence to this idea is the so-called 'string theory,' which suggests that behind the atomic structure of matter are very subtle vibrations that give that structure its life, quality, rhythm, and form. The origins of these vibrations, scientists say, are small energy-particles linked together in strands. These vibrating 'strings,' are all made up of the same basic energy-substance. The shapes, which these vibrating strands take, determine the nature, type, and quality of the substance they produce. According to the mathematics used to substantiate this so-called 'theory of everything,' these shapes are multidimensional.

In many areas the findings of science confirm the teachings of the initiates. An interesting book might be written comparing and bringing together these two slowly merging approaches to the truth, scientific and direct perception. When the scientific community begins to seriously investigate psychic energy, the creative power of thought, then perhaps it will be discovered that the vibrating keynote of things can be influenced by this subtle energy. And if by the same token the psychic community will begin to experiment and verify its findings, then perhaps an open-minded approach to science and a scientific approach to spiritual matters may ensue.

In 1787, physicist Ernst Chladni published a book called *Discoveries Concerning the Theory of Music*, in which he laid the foundations for acoustics, the science of sound. Among his discoveries was the fact that sound vibrations have shape and are form producing. He demonstrated this by drawing a violin bow perpendicularly across the edge of a flat plate covered with sand. The sound patterns that this produced are today known as the Chladni figures.

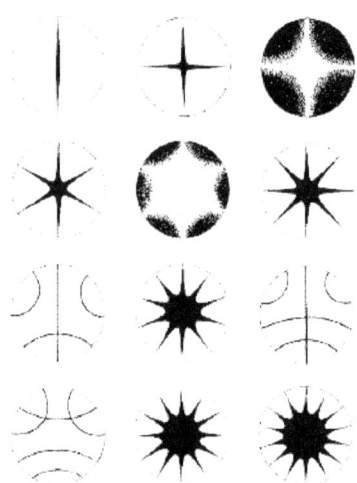

According to Rudolf Steiner we can train ourselves clairvoyantly to see and feel the forms that the sounds of the alphabet naturally makes when uttered. It is the form making property of sound, he says, which the *Elohim* used during creation.

When the sound of A moves through the air, learn to feel not merely its tone, learn to feel the form it makes, just as the tone of the violin bow, passed over the edge of a plate, makes a form in the powder. Learn to feel the A and the B in their transience through space. Learn to experience them not merely as sound but as form producing. This is a thoroughly objective language, which if the soul is receptive, is crystallized into pictures as the sounds are uttered. The pictures that crowd upon the soul of the seer when he enters into the supersensible world originate from that lofty discipline which perceives the crystallization of sounds. Sound in this way is transmuted into spiritual form appearing before the soul as pictures that form a connected whole.... These forms are the very pictures that one perceives when one penetrates to the supersensible and out of which our material physical has evolved.[1]

In 1967 the Swiss Doctor Hans Jenny, following in Chladni's footsteps, made what he called the tonoscope, a device that makes the human voice visible by vibrating a metal plate filled with sand. He demonstrated that every physical sound has a corresponding geometric pattern.

The vowel A in sand

---

[1] From a lecture given August 18, 1910

The sound pattern said to be of the vowel A.

This science, which he called Cymatics, demonstrates how vibrations are in fact form producing. A. S. Raleigh, in his *Science of Motion of Number* has this to say on the subject of vibration:

> All forms of energy are in a continuous state of vibration. The cosmic energy, with its ultimate atom, is vibrating to a certain rhythm. This rhythm holds the energy of the atom together. The atom, by reason of this rhythm, assumes a certain form— a definite geometrical figure. It also expresses itself in a definite color and produces a definite sound, by reason of its rhythmic vibration.[1]

By applying the Law of Analogy it could also be demonstrated that the subtle vibrations of thought (psychic-energy) are, in the same way, form producing. This idea is confirmed in the Agni Yoga Teaching.

> The projection of thought upon a highly sensitized film is quite possible, but for this one should collect the most acute thinking. The chief thing lies in the quality of thinking. Sound creates rhythm upon the sand. Thought also emits vibrations. But of course, it is much finer than sound. Therefore thought cannot react upon the coarse grains of sand but does act upon the delicate film.[2]

In the same way that a clear musical note will produce geometric patterns in sand, so do the vibrations of clear thought produce corresponding patterns in the ethers. Some interesting experiments along this line can be found in Jule Eiesnbud's remarkable book, *The World of Ted Serios: Thoughtographic Studies of an Extraordinary Mind*. By

---

[1] *The Science of Motin and Number*. By A.S. Raligh, page 9.

[2] *Heart* 439

visualizing a scene in his mind he could transfer that image to the film in a camera.

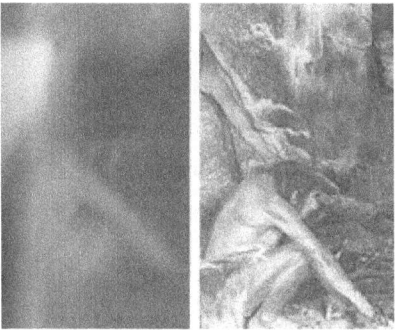

Recently Japanese scientist Masaru Emoto demonstrated that thoughts and emotions can effect the shape of water molecules in the same way that sound can effect sand in a dish. Fresh spring water when frozen while being subjected to directed thought and feelings produces certain patterns in the frozen ice.

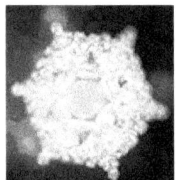
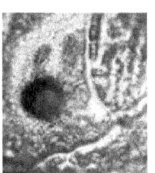
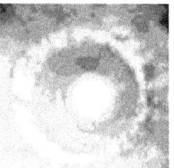

Feelings of Gratitude   Polluted Water   Distilled Water

This experiment is useful as long as we remember that when using ice crystals as the screen upon which patterns of thought are projected they are being viewed through the already existing six-pointed geometrical patterns of the element of water itself. In other words the basic geometry of the images obtained in this way will be primarily that of water and only secondarily express the pattern of the emotion or thought projected upon it.

In the same way that a saturated chemical solution will naturally form crystal patterns in a dish, so the saturation of space with thought will naturally produce crystals of light substance in mental substance (*chitta*), which can be projected into etheric matter. The clairvoyant seer perceives the effects of subtle thought vibrations as patterns of light.[1] It is the most fundamental of these subtle light-images that form the basis for the Sensa language. Sensa then is the visual and audible correspondences to the fundamental patterns of thought as they arise from higher archetypal patterns of being.

The ancient Mystery Schools taught that the material universe arose from the Archetypal Mind reflecting itself through creative seed-patterns that were understood and acted upon by the creative Gods and nature spirits. Each of these fundamental patterns has its own glyph or sign, which accurately depicts its essential nature. For those who know how to read this Language of the Gods, the geometric signs reveal metaphysical truths with mathematical accuracy. Rudolf Steiner called this 'meta-geometry.' Unlike Euclidean geometry, which merely measures physical space, esoteric geometry measures metaphysical space. Steiner applied metaphysical geometry primarily to the etheric plane, but it can be applied to psychic energy just as well. The Pythagoreans applied their meta-geometry to the 'Science of the Spheres,' or astrology. Astrology, from the perspective of the Temple Brethren, is a science that maps the cyclic descent of those evolutionary currents that the solar and planetary Gods bring to bear to further the destiny of the world. Geometry as it applies to astrology demonstrates the unique relationships that exist between these currents at any point in time.

In the 1960's Buckminster Fuller, one of the great original thinkers of the twentieth century, discovered that the physical and non-physical universes conform to the same fundamental laws and principles. The creative process of thought, he tells us, follows the same laws of form production as the growth of physical organisms. Thought, he says, is a consciousness sorting process that takes mental

---

[1] See Leadbeater's *Thought Forms*.

objects and combines them into form. And like all organic form-producing processes, the formulation of thoughts and ideas take place along certain geometric lines of interconnected relationships. The process of thought, says Fuller, can best be understood by viewing the mind as a sphere with the observer at the center.

Within this mental sphere conscious experiences are sorted along geometric lines. The most basic pattern needed for the formation of a complete thought, says Fuller, is the tetrahedron.

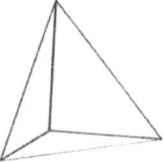

Using this geometric model fuller demonstrated that no fewer than four experiences, depicted by the four triangles, and six relationships between them, demonstrated by the lines of force, are required for a complete thought. From this simple pattern more complex patterns of thought can be constructed.

Fuller was particularly interested in discovering the geometric relationships and correspondences that exist between the form-building activity of the human mind and the form-building activity of nature. He extended this line of inquiry to include the geometric correspondences that exist between the thought process itself and the essential principles that produce and maintain intelligence. By understanding the natural patterns of these relationships, he said, we can learn to support and even further the harmonious development and evolution of these patterns in the world. We can then learn to create forms in the physical universe that correspond to those naturally occurring in the nonphysical universe. This, he said, is humanity's mission and much of his writing, including his magnum opus, *Synergetics: Explorations in the Geometry of Thinking*, deals with the application of the natural geometry of thought to the ideal construction of these patterns upon the physical plane. According to Fuller when the physically created forms conform to the innate archetypal patterns of the mind they will be beautiful. In this Fuller, who was definitely an original thinker, was echoing the secret Hermetic and Platonic doctrine exactly.

A portion of the evolution of the human thought process can be observed, says Fuller, in the evolution of 20th century popular music. Because of his heightened sense of hearing Fuller could sense on a large scale the basic sound patterns behind the music he heard. From this he could correlate popular music geometrically with the evolutionary transformations that were taking place in the cultural environment, particularly those that relate to science and technology. In this way he was able to trace the patterns of human thinking through its music to the fundamental changes taking place in the general culture. A remarkable achievement! He recommended that we make use of geodesic domes for living because its form corresponds with the natural geometry of intelligence and was therefore in-step with the natural evolution of consciousness.

In the Mystery Schools it was taught that each thought produces a complicated geometric form that has the power to manifest its corresponding likeness into form upon the physical plane. Paul Christian (1811-1877) writes:

> When the soul creates (evokes a thought) the representative signs of that thought is self-engraved upon the astral fluid, which acts as a mirror for the manifestations of being.[1]

Plato states in his *Dialogue on Nature (Timaeus)* that the five-polyhedron solids—the dodecahedron, octahedron, Tetrahedron, Icosahedron, and the cube represent in the sphere of divine Intelligence (*Nous*) the five primary seed-patterns of the physical universe. Each of these archetypal hieroglyphs are reflected in manifestation as the five elements—earth, water, fire, air, and ether.

---

[1] Pierre Christian. *Histoire de la Magie et du Monde Surnaturel.* Quoted by H.P. Blavatsky.

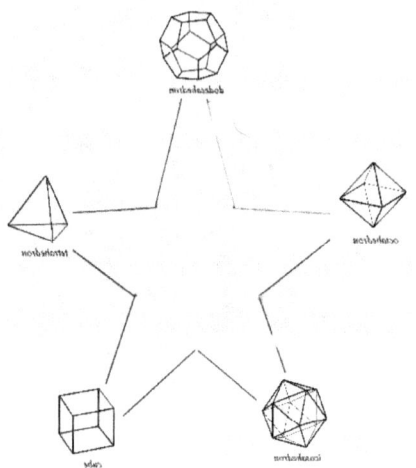

The Pythagoreans, including Plato, symbolically represented the five elements with the pentad. The geometrical archetype of fifth element of aether, the Dodecahedron, was considered the synthesis of the other elements and therefore placed at the apex of the pentagram. The Pythagoreans called this unity of the elements—Nature.[1]

Esoteric Hinduism also uses five geometric forms to represent the same five archetypal patterns of the mind and their reflection in the five elements on the physical plane though in simplified two dimensional forms: the point, crescent, triangle, circle and the square. There is a definite correspondence between the two systems.

---

[1] See Manly Hall's *Secret Teachings of all Ages*, page LXX, lower left.

Point	Ether	Dodecahedron
Crescent	Air	Octahedron
Triangle	Fire	Tetrahedron
Circle	Water	Icosahedron
Square	Earth	Cube

The secret tradition of the Bards of the Isle of Britain, as recorded in the Welch manuscript *Barddas* in 1862, names the five elements as 'earth, water, sky, fire, and nyv" or ether. "The nyv is of God and life. It is intelligent. From the first four arise death and mortality. From the fifth arises all life and motion." Nyv, also spelled neph, is synonymous with the Egyptian cneph or that which pervades and animates the whole world.

In Buddhist symbolism these five geometric forms correspond to the five levels of a stupa.

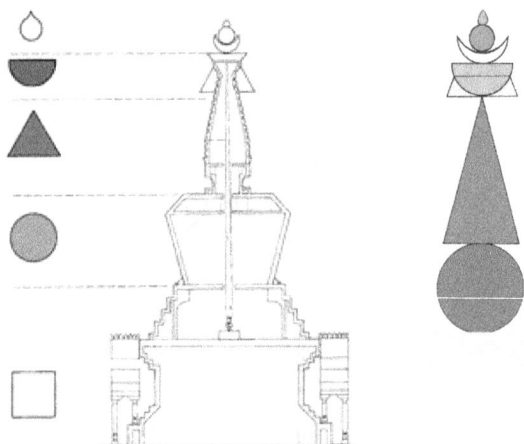

Each of the elements, ether, air, fire, water, and earth, also represents a level of consciousness sometimes referred to as the 'five wisdoms.' Esoterically these five principles are seven.[1] This can be seen in crescent, circle, and drop at the top of the stupa thus extending the five into seven.

D. K. has hinted, more than once, that one of the ways in which the seven principles can be accurately divided is to picture the third or manas aspect of the atma-buddhi-manas tri-unity as the synthesizing point for the lower four, creating thereby a pentagram descending from the sacred three. H. P. Blavatsky has given us a visual model for this idea, which we will examine more closely later.

---

[1] According the H.P. Blavatsky the reason why many esoteric systems depict the principles as 5 instead of 7 is because 5 are manifested and two highest are not yet manifested. See her *The Secret Doctrine* 1st edition, page 108.

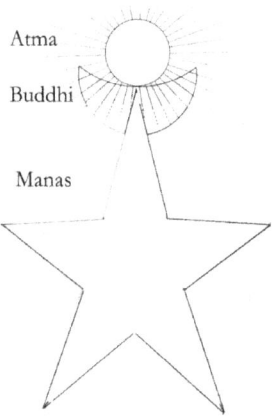

Atma

Buddhi

Manas

"Manas," writes D. K., "is the synthetic vibration of the five rays," the major third and minor four."[1] The synthesis of the lower four vehicles into manas or universal mind, so that they can act as a single coordinated unit, occurs we are told, at initiation into the Greater Mysteries. The symbol for this initiation is the Flaming Star, the divine pentagram, which represents the WORD as the Mind manifesting a portion of itself along with its purpose into the mind stream and activity of the initiate. The WORD descends upon the initiate, we are told, through the great Flaming Diamond or Rod of Power, welded by the Hierophant at the time of initiation. "The five-pointed star," writes Brother D.K., "at the time of initiation on the mental plane flashes out above the head of the initiate."[2] It represents psychic energy, the fire of mind, the point of origin of the 'lower four' maya reflections that are synthesized at initiation. The pentagram is the symbol of the Adept who has fully united the 'lower four' energies with their essential nature, the higher Mind.

Brother D.K. and Rudolf Steiner agree that the pentagram, on the physical plane, can accurately depict the physical-etheric body of a human being. D.K. states:

[1] *A Treatise on Cosmic Fire*, page 308 also see page 336.

[2] *A Treatise on Cosmic Fire* page 696

This five fold nature of the dense physical body is brought about through the fact that only five centers are really active in average man up to the third initiation; all are there and all are vitalized, but only five in this five fold normal evolution are dominant. The force of these five, therefore, sweeps the dense substance into a close aggregation. As two of the centres are not functioning as actively as the other five an ovoid is not formed as in the case of the etheric, astral and mental sheaths. The fivefold shape of physical man is the result of the fivefold direction of force currents from five centres.[1]

Of course the pentagram like all aspects of esoteric geometry can be approached from many corresponding levels.

The lost science of *mantra-yantra* also deals with the natural vibrational and geometrical relationships that exist between the mind and from. Visual patterns and rhythmic sounds are two ways of perceiving and describing mental phenomena. Both are symbolic and somewhat inadequate attempts to express the patterns and interconnectedness of the laws and principles involved.

Rudolf Steiner says that esoteric script "coordinates the lines of force which streams creatively form the WORD, forming itself into definite figures and colour forms." 'The lines of force streaming from the WORD,' the divine manifestation of universal Mind, are evolutionary currents that descend from the heavenly spheres. D. K. gives the following hint concerning the connection between these streams and esoteric symbols:

> These streams [of cosmic energy] pass in different directions, and in the knowledge of occult direction comes knowledge of the various hierarchies of being and the secret of esoteric symbols.[2]

---

[1] A Treatise on Cosmic Fire, pages 790-791.
[2] *A Treatise on Cosmic Fire* by Alice Bailey, page 1183.

'Occult direction' here means the lines of force, which the incoming currents take when stepped down through the various hierarchies of our planetary system or individually through the various centers of the etheric body. These evolutionary streams or 'Rays' give impulse and direction to the evolution of consciousness and spirit. The individual configurations that these currents produce in time as they pass through the various hierarchies in rhythmic sequence of ever greater and lesser 'turns of the spiral' can be charted geometrically. D.K. Continues:

> All these streams of [cosmic] energy form geometrical designs of great beauty to the eyes of the initiated seer. We have the transverse and bisecting lines, the seven lines of force which form the planes and the seven spiraling lines, thus forming lines of systemic latitude and longitude, and their interplay and interaction produce a whole of wondrous beauty and design.[1]

Albert Einstein in his very readable *Evolution of Physics*, which he wrote with Leopold Infeld, shows how geometric images were used in science to depict the lines of force of electromagnetic currents.

> It would be rather difficult to describe this force in words. Even a mathematical formula would be complicated and awkward. It is best to represent all we know about the acting force by a drawing, or rather a spatial model, with lines of force.[2]

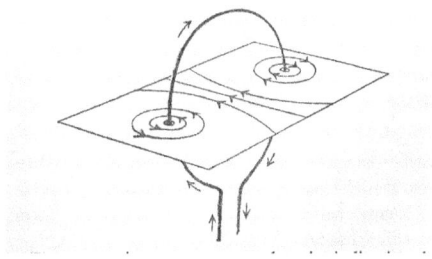

---

[1] Page 1184.
[2] *Evolution of Physics*, page 133

The current passing through a closed circuit will always produce a magnetic field with its own lines of force circulating (spiraling) perpendicular to electric current. The simplest model is the field of the bar magnet or a simple electric current, both of which produce the same two-pole magnetic field. Electrical energy moves from one point to another. Magnetic energy radiates out from a center.

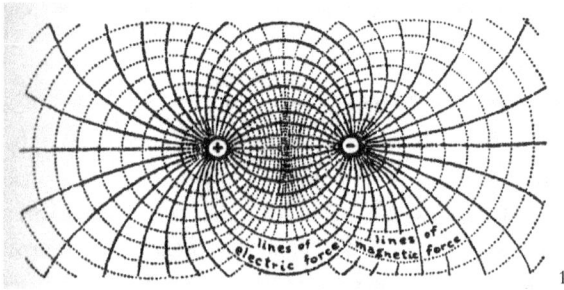

Initiates and physicists basically agree — All is energy. And if we apply the Hermetic axiom 'as above, so below,' the principles of the polarity of energy lie at the very heart of all activity on all levels— atomic, chemical, electrical, biological, social, psychic, planetary and cosmic. "As psychic energy is an energy it will not contradict the laws of physics."[2] Through the interaction of the magnetic poles radiation occurs creating a field of energy. All forms, whether physical or conceptual, arise within the fields created by interaction of polar opposites.

[1] This diagram is taken form Lawrence Blair's remarkable book *Rhythms of Vision*. Schocken Books, 1976
[2] *Heart*

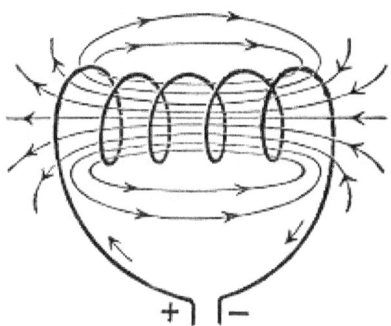

What is not yet generally recognized is that all natural polarities are balanced by third point, as a fulcrum, upon a higher level, thereby forming a subtle triangle of energies. This is the basis for the symbolism of the triangle—unity and duality considered as a whole.

To demonstrate the patterns produced by the interaction of three or more centers geometrically we must remember that each point represents the *central* point around which the lesser lives, which together make up the whole organism, revolve.

As we have stated the shapes of the Sensa characters are determined by the patterns that arise from lines of force moving between the centers of any living whole system (monad).

According to Plato one of the reasons why the study of geometry is so important is that it elevates the mind out of the world of the senses. Only by removing the mind from the influence of sense perception can we enter the higher realm of archetypal Ideas. Quoting Plato, Rudolf Steiner writes:

> *"Through mathematics you can learn to liberate yourself from the senses and rise to the comprehension of Idea-forms [Eidos] independently of the senses."*

This was what Plato strove to impress upon his disciples. The Gnostics desired something similar. They said, *"Gnosis is*

Mathesis." They did not mean by this that the essence of the world can be based on mathematical ideas, but only that the first stages in the spiritual education of Man are constituted by what is supersensible in mathematical thought. When a man reaches the stage of being able to think of other properties of the world independently of sense-perception he is then able to think mathematically in geometrical forms and in the arithmetical relations of numbers. Then he is fairly on the path to spiritual knowledge. They did not strive for Mathesis [mathematics] as such, but rather for supersensible knowledge *after the pattern* of Mathesis. They regarded Mathesis as a model or a prototype, because the geometrical proportions of the World are the most elementary and simple, and such as Man can most easily understand. He must learn through the elementary mathematical truths to become emancipated from sense in order that he may reach, later, the point where the higher problems are appropriately to be considered. This will certainly mean, for many, a giddy height of human perceptive faculties. Those, however, who may be considered as true Occultists have in every age demanded from their disciples the courage to make this giddy height their goal: — *"Learn to think of the essence of Nature and of Spiritual Being as being independent of sense-perception. As the mathematician thinks of the circle and its laws, so you may become a student of Occult Science"* — this is what everyone who really seeks after Truth should keep before his mind as if written in letters of gold. *"You will never find in the world perceived by the senses, a circle that will not confirm for you what thou hast learned about the circle understood by supersensible mathematical perception. No experience will ever contradict your supersensible perception. Thus do you gain for yourself an imperishable and eternal knowledge when you learn to perceive free of the senses."* In this way did Plato, the Gnostics and all Occultists conceive mathematical science as an educational means.[1]

_____

[1] From a lecture entitled Mathematics and Occultism given June 21, 1904.

Buckminster Fuller applied geometry toward mapping of those natural force currents of psychic energy needed to produce the activity of thought. Fuller called this 'the primary geometry of thought.'

Rudolf Steiner used geometry to map the natural 'formative forces' of etheric space. This is illustrated by two very remarkable books based upon the writings of Rudolf Steiner, *The Plant Between Sun and Earth* by George Adams and Olive Whicher and *Sunspace* by Olive Whicher. Along with Steiner's *The Fourth Dimension* these books are excellent studies of esoteric geometry from the perspective of the etheric plane. Geometry was one of the requirements for students seeking to enter the school established by Pythagoras.

Sir John Woodroffe, in his *Garland of Letters,* a work on the metaphysics of the Sanskrit alphabet in its relation to mantra, states, "The true and natural name of something arises from the subtle sounds produced by the motion of its essential nature on the plane of mind." This idea, which also forms the basis for the lost twilight language (*Samdhyabhashya*) of ancient India, applies equally well to Sensa or Sensar as H. P. Blavatsky called it. According to her Sensar, the *Samdhyabhashya*, and the language of the Mysteries are one and the same.

The Teacher states: "Every letter in a word transmits vibration by its sound and these vibrations effect the centers." When there is a direct concordance between the sound, the thought, and its inherent meaning the mantra will have a powerful effect.

The Sanskrit term 'mantra' is derived from the root 'man,' meaning 'to think.' Woodroffe quotes an ancient tantra shastra that says, "Mantra is so called because it is primarily a mental process." The effectiveness of the science of mantra lies not only in the physical sounds but in the use of psychic energy, the power of thought, colored by those higher vibration that correspond to the created sounds. *The Shiva Sutra,* which according to legend was written by the great Mahadeva Himself, says, "Mantra is of the mind."[1] In the esoteric scriptures of India spiritual sound or vibration (*Sabda)* is of two kinds,

---

[1] 2:1

subtle and dense. Mantra therefore can be sounded on two levels, vocally (*Japa*) and mentally (*Ajapa*). Both the Hindu and Buddhist scriptures agree, the greater of the two ways to sound a mantra is with the mind alone. Subtle Sabda is considered real while its audible correspondent is but a reflection, a mirage, a maya. "The AUM," says Brother D.K., "when rightly used by the soul on the *mental plane* vitalizes and expedites all thought-forms, and so produces successful enterprise." [1] According to H. P. Blavatsky the Lost Word was "pronounced mentally by initiated priests."[2] The power of mantra lies not in a mindless repetition of syllables but with the power of the mind focused, as a 'point of tension,' upon the inner meaning, producing those rhythmic vibrations of thought that correspond to the intended result.

The Arhats tell us that what we call the natural world perceived by the senses is but a reflection of the vibrating rhythmic patterns of light taking place upon the higher levels of the mental plane. These original patterns, when known and understood, can be accurately expressed as the true language of nature on the mental plane only when its vibrations match the original impulse. To accomplish this we must first understand the difference between those impulses that originate from our own desire-emotional nature and those that descend from the higher worlds. Secondly we need to perceive the natural correspondences that exist between spiritual impulses and their manifestation in form. The *Kalachakratantra* gives a few hints in this area. It instructs the yogi to tune in to, rather than merely to sound, the vibrating seed syllables (*bija*) of the different nerve centers. [3] For example, by using the sound vibration of the heart center as an object of meditation the yogi seeks to merge the consciousness with the essence of that energy. The subtle vibrations of the centers, when viewed clairvoyantly appear as geometric symbols. This is true of the

---

[1] *A Treatise on White Magic*, p. 478

[2] *Isis Unveiled* Vol. I, xliv

[3] 2. 116

essential vibrations of all living organisms, great or small. The number of petals of a given center is a hint to its geometric form.

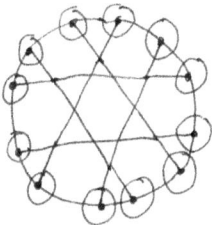

To prepare the yogi for the seeing, hearing, and utilizing these subtle vibrations he is instructed to visualize their *bijas,* their archetypal seed patterns, as they are pictorially depicted by the alphabet of his or her own language. Thus, while this may veil the true shapes of these subtle sound vibrations, it can also prompt (invoke) the higher corresponding esoteric script to arise in the mind stream.

> Verily, manifold and intricate as the most delicate design are the manifestations of psychic energy. What beautiful images will be perceptible to the enlightened eye.[1]

"Thought," says the Teacher, "creates a special fiery substance."[2] This substance takes shape according to the nature and quality of our thoughts. When the thoughts are directly expressing the realization of higher truth the light-patterns will be beautiful. When our thoughts are not in step with the natural evolution of consciousness ugly distorted thought-images are the result. This often leads to other problems.

> A Thought corresponding to reality forms a vehicle for an elemental. Everything worthy, austere, vital, gravitates toward creative thought and will beneficently sustain its creator. But the devices of slander will attract brooding elementals, who, failing

---

[1] *Agni Yoga* 554
[2] *Fiery World* II 380.

to find a vital foundation, will precipitate themselves upon the slanderer.[1]

Thoughts and feelings produce subtle sound vibrations, which are either in harmony or not with evolution.

> In the human organism rhythm and harmony lie dormant. We must awaken them for this music must become a part, an important part, of our education... The sound may be inaudible like the heart's tension, for it is the heart that sings. It resounds and fills the organism with special energy. The prayer itself, AUM, may also be in the heart, but it engenders radiations, as does an uttered sound.[2]

One of the primary ingredients in sounding a mantra correctly is its concordance with the realization of its essential meaning.

> But a sound may be rightly understood and still produce no results. Therefore, let us not forget the heart's energy, which must accompany the sound.[3]

The primary power of mantra is not so much in the physical sounds that are produced, which are secondary, but in the much subtler corresponding vibrations of thought and feeling. And if we add to this a rhythmic striving, will, and the visual archetype of the intended vibration we will have a powerful tool to hasten the natural evolution of consciousness.

According to Madam Blavatsky, as well as some of the more esoteric schools of India, each letter of the Sanskrit alphabet has an individual and fundamental esoteric meaning. It also has a corresponding geometrical form that has always been kept secret from the uninitiated. These visual geometric forms, which are called *yantras*, are the vibrational signatures of those great spiritual beings who

---

[1] *Fiery World* I, 428.

[2] *AUM*

[3] *AUM* 50

embody the original fundamental principles or truths which they represent. And although much of the original meaning of these yantras has been lost or distorted over time, and in most cases withdrawn from public eye, there are still a few key elements available that might be considered. Y*antra*, like the Sensa alphabet to which it is related, is a science depicting through simplified diagrams the higher pictorial archetype of those seed-vibrations (*bijas*) that are expressed by a *mantra*. The most important yantras in esoteric Hinduism are those depicting the sixteen *Nityas*. The Nityas represent fundamental principles that do not change:

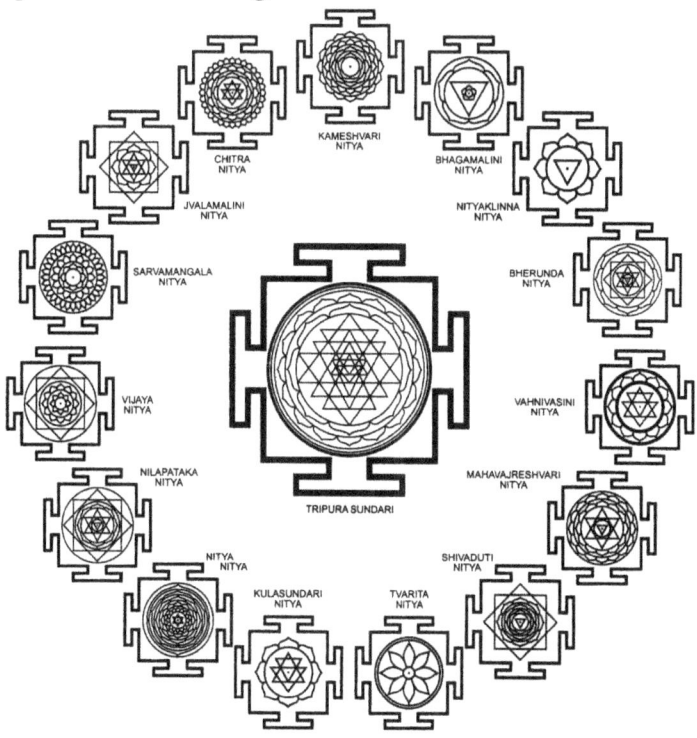

According to the Abhinavagupta's *Tantraraja* each *Nitya* corresponds to one of the 16 vowels of the Sanskrit alphabet beginning with the *Kameshavari Nitya* and following the natural steps of creation (manifestation) clockwise around the wheel of time (*Kalachakra*). The reversed wheel, which progresses counterclockwise beginning with *Chritra Nitya*, follows the path of evolution, also known as the Path of Return (*Nivrittimarga*). It represents the progressive stages in the natural evolution of consciousness back to its primary source at the center. As Abhinavagupta points out in his monumental *Paratrisika Vivarana* the vowel sounds each have a different, though corresponding, meaning depending upon the direction in which the wheel is turning. The *Book of Light (Zohar)* states that God created the world by sounding the primordial alphabet in the reverse order.

Divine signatures, when made public, are nearly always given in a veiled form, condensed from the original in such a way that only those students with an awakened intuition and therefore ready and able to use the information responsibly, will understand fully. To decipher these forms, to fill in some of the missing pieces, the following points might be useful:

1. Each symbol is the signature of a living being, which like all beings, are made up of lesser beings as cells within their body of expression.

2. Each of the petals of a flower (or points of a star or triangle) depicts the orbit of a negatively polarized life around its positive center.

3. The points of the petals, triangles or stars are the central points of other invisible circles.

4. A complete geometric signature of a being, truth, or principle will always depict in some way the three levels of being, corresponding to spirit, consciousness and essential form.

According to the *Shiva Sutras* [1] the source of all things in manifestation, including basic truths, laws and principles, are those archetypal thought vibrations that originate from the plane of mind.

---

[1] There are several excellent translations in English of this important work. One of the best is by Mark S. G. Dyczkowdki. It contains the Bhaskara commentary. *The Aphorisms of Siva,* State Univ. of New York Press, 1992.

Sanskrit vowel sounds represent the most fundamental of these bijas (thought vibrations). The secret of the science of mantra/yantra, which creatively channels the power of psychic energy, is found in the correspondence that exists between the seed syllables, the seed geometric forms, and the seed thought vibrations sounded upon the mental plane. The term 'seed,' like all seeds, pertains to the archetypal pattern behind its manifestation in form. In the Sanskrit alphabet vowels are said to represent the most fundamental unchanging principles (*nityas*), while the consonants, which cannot be pronounced or manifest without the vowel sounds which stand behind them, are the seed vibrations behind those secondary principles in Nature that to some degree change over time. Primary Sanskrit seed-syllables or *bijas* are nearly always made up entirely of vowel sounds.

As each of the principles involved in life on the sphere is embodied by a living being the letters of the Sanskrit alphabet are sometimes called '*Matrika*,' or 'little mothers,' while *Matri Tripurasundari*, the Great Mother Herself, depicted at the center, embodies them all as a synthesis of the manifested universe.[1]

To understand the meaning of the 16 *Nityas* and their correspondences with the 16 vowels of the Sanskrit alphabet we must remember that much of original meaning depicted in their ancient Sanskrit names have for the most part been lost or kept secret. We should also understand that on the 'reversed wheel,' the upward evolutionary spiral, the meanings have a different directional meaning from those on the downward involutionary arch. To retrieve their true meaning, therefore, an intuitive approach will be useful, such as that adopted by Abhinavagupta in his masterwork the *Paratrisika Vivarana*.

In the same way that certain musical notes or chords can invoke definite feelings in those that hear them, so can vowel and consonant sounds evoke definite feelings and even mental images when contemplated upon. If we can penetrate to the root source of these images and feel the vibrations that they create or invoke in us, we can begin to understand intuitively their essential meaning.

Concerning the pictorial symbolic nature of the original Sanskrit alphabet K. C. Aryan, in his book *The Little Goddesses*, writes:

In the earliest form of worship of the Hindu gods and goddesses, pictorial symbols were drawn in the middle of circles and triangles. This combination of pictorial symbols and geometrical forms gave birth the Devanagari script. These pictorial symbols have been termed variously as ancient sacred writing or hieroglyphics or ideograms, which are the earliest form of Sanskrit alphabets. The letters (*Varna*) of the Devanagari script have the names of the hieroglyphics. The belief or supposition that the Sanskrit alphabets originated form the city of the gods (*Devanam Nagaram*), as mentioned in the Taittiriya Upanishad, is not superficial or meaningless, for it implies that the letters emanated from the hieroglyphics or ideograms which had appropriated to themselves the names of Hindu gods and goddesses.[1]

The original pictorial and geometrical symbols of the Sanskrit alphabet can be discovered, not so much from a study of ancient Tantric literature, which is not always reliable, but, as Rudolf Steiner suggests, by letting the sounds of the letters work upon us in such a way that their inner form natures becomes apparent in the consciousness. But in this we must first remove the academic prejudice that views all subjective evidence as unworthy of consideration. When studying a sacred language such as Sanskrit or Hebrew we must remember that words pertaining to higher levels of truth are synthetic in their meaning. In other words they combine truths that would normally be considered as separate ideas into an intrinsic whole. Therefore when considering the fundamental meaning of the individual Sanskrit letters (particularly the vowels) we must understand that the names that are given must be understood in terms of a higher synthesis. Arthur Avalon rightly points out in his *Garland of Letters* that the fundamental sound syllables of a mantra only 'approximately' represent their counterparts on the higher planes. Rudolf Steiner confirms this by noting that the colors and sounds of the physical world are only the lower correspondence of their true nature on the higher planes.

The Sanskrit and Hebrew languages, though the meanings of the words have undoubtedly changed over time, are nevertheless derived from and correspond to some degree *in sound* to the same one original sacred tongue. Steiner writes:

---

[1] Page 18, Rekha Pakashan, 1980

The Hebrew Tongue is a language that works upon the soul quite differently from any modern language. Although the Hebrew of the early chapters of Genesis may not perhaps have the same effect today, at one time it worked in such a way that when a letter was sounded it called up a picture in the soul. The Hebrew language, *or more accurately the language with which the first chapters of Genesis was written,*[1] enabled the soul to call up picture images which were not wholly unlike those that are presented to the seer when, freed from his body, he is able to look into supersensible regions of existence.

Some of the sound equivalences of Sensa can be found in the Sanskrit and Hebrew languages as well as in the alphabets of most countries. The geometrical – pictorial aspects, though taught in the Mystery Schools, have remained hidden (esoteric) from the public. This is because the yantra, or visual aspect, when combined with its mantra or sound counterpart makes the 'words of power' very powerful. The magical use of these words of power is dangerous. It self-mastery has not been attained the invoked elementals, or nature spirits, can easily stimulate the form side of our nature and imprison the worker in the chains of maya. Moksha, we must remember, is liberation from all outside conditioning.

In the secret archives of the Brotherhood there is an ancient manuscript. It contains six mysterious formulas "written in words, symbols, and symbolic forms" on "six large sheet of an unknown mental." These formulas represent those truths that need to be realized, embodied, and applied before taking one or other of the initiations into the Mysteries. By 'sounding' the necessary formulas correctly the neophyte can approach a realization of the meaning and significance of his next step forward on the Path. The term 'sounding,' does not mean speaking or chanting, but rather to create the necessary vibration. D. K. says that the "building patterns" that are to be mastered are "essentially the geometric forms lying behind all

---

[1] Blavatsky says that portions of Genesis were originally written in the Mystery language.

160

exoteric manifestations; even when presented in words and phrases they are susceptible of being reduced to definite [geometric] forms."[1] While training one of his disciples in the art of visual mental telepathy, sent to him telepathically two geometric symbols. He was instructed to 'contact the symbols' during meditation and then to discover thereby the corresponding words that belong to it.[2] Rudolf Steiner writes of this:

> Reading the esoteric script involves not only the seeing of isolated pictures but the letting of the interrelationship of these pictures work upon one.[3]

The vibrations produced by accurately 'sounding' the sacred names can be enhanced through certain ritual ceremonies. Adepts and initiates of the Mysteries, by arranging themselves in certain rhythmically moving geometric formations, can invoke thereby cosmic energies for the benefit of the world. The great Wesak festival (Vaisakha), which takes place on the full moon in May, is one such ritual.[4] Iamblichus, in his monumental treatise, *On the Egyptian Mysteries,* explains the essential nature of the ceremonies as enacted in the Mysteries:

> The ceremonies of the Mysteries are presented in direct concordance with those wonderful signatures that descend from *Demiurgus* [Creator] through both the mental and celestial Hierarchy of Gods. This divine descent is in line with the eternal evolution of all beings. Through the Hierarchy of Gods things of an ineffable nature are unfolded into light through arcane

---

[1] *Discipleship in the New Age* Vol. 2, p. 363

[2] *Discipleship in the New Age* Vol. I, p. 305

[3] *Rosicrucian Wisdom* p. 16

[4] According to calculations made by the great Tibetan scholar Milpam from his reading of the *Kalachakra Tantra,* this now occurs in the astrological sign of Aries. This may not be the contradiction it seems for due to the procession of the equinox the sun at the spring equinox is now at entering the sign of Aquarius and therefore passes through the sign of Arise for the greater part in the month of May. Also see *A Treatise on White Magic,* Page 437, second paragraph.

symbols. These symbol-forms veil the formless. The greatest things, therefore, are expressed through those images that have divine causes and are so divorced from the sphere of the [human] psyche that mere reason cannot reach them.

In one sense, says Iamblichus, these symbolic images "possess the same power as the gods themselves."[1] Another example of this can be found in the ritual of the holy Eucharist established by the Apostle Paul in the esoteric school he established in Athens. Dionysius the Areopagite, a student of that school and as Steiner tells us, the father of esoteric Christianity, tells us that the ritual of the holy Eucharist is "communion with the divine leading to union with the divine." To Dionysius the Eucharist ritual is a symbolic enactment of Initiation into the "Holy Mysteries."

> Every sacredly initiated operation of the Eucharist draws our fragmented lives together into a unified spiritualization. It creates a divine unity out of the divisions within us. It grants us communion and union with the One.[2] The Sacrament of the Divine Birth is of the first [initiation], which introduces us to the spiritual light, the source of all divine illumination. And while it is true that all of the initiations of the Hierarchy have this in common, to pass the light of God on to the initiates, it was this one that first gave me the gift of sight. The light coming from this first [initiation] led me toward the vision of other sacred things. The objective of the sacred initiations is to impart the mysteries of Deity to the one being initiated. The Hierarchy has given to each a name, or sign, to signify the essential nature of what is being achieved.

H. P. Blavatsky stated that there were some Theosophists of her time who understood the 'Mystery-language.' One of them, she said,

---

[1] Iamblichus *De Mysteries* Translated by Emma Clarke, John Dillon and Jackson Hershbell, page 61, ABL 2003

[2] See his *Ecclesiastical Hierarchy*, chapter 3.

had contributed articles anonymously to some of the early Theosophical magazines. One such early contributor, who identifies himself simply as 'A Brahmin,' veils the Mystery-language thus:

> The World Song, obeying certain laws of proportions of Pythagorean arithmetic and imparting its thrilling effect to the domain of cosmic substance, has induced the latter into a crystallization process that the philosopher Plato called the geometry of the cosmos. The various forms that are observed from a molecule of salt crystal to the wonderfully complex organism of the human body are all the structures of the great cosmic geometriser known as Viswakarma, the deva carpenter of our Puranic writings. The revealed Veda whose function is to trace out the cosmos from one basic sound substance symbolized as OM necessarily split itself into a primal three, a subsequent seven vowels, and then into seven notes and then into seven combinations of the seven notes [49] on a basic three and then into [the Vedic] hymns. All these falling into the material field of the consonants, gradually produced the manifested crystallized forms, which are collectively taken as the universe.[1]

We must remember that when initiates use the term 'sound' it often has a higher significance than the sound that is registered by the ears. When the vibrations of archetypal ideas, laws, and principles are represented as notes on a keyboard, or as colors of the visible spectrum, we should understand that they only correspond to physical plane sounds and colors. The same can be said for those geometrical symbols that correspond to the archetypal vibrations. The WORD descends into form through a crystallization of its subtle vibrations. Each condensation has its own geometric patterns. These patterns show the primary lines of descent along with the essential nature of the

---

[1] *Some Thoughts on the Gita* by A Brahmin, (1893) reprinted by the Eastern School Press 1983. This passage was quoted by Alice Bailey many times as footnotes in Brother D.K.'s *A Treatise on Cosmic Fire.*

forms and principles to be manifested. The closer they get to the physical sphere the more complicated they become. The Sensa alphabet is a stylized depiction of these geometric vibrations as they appear to the awakened inner perception while they are still in their mental seed-forms and before they descend to the physical plane.

Sensa Script

In sight of the sacred signs my barren thoughts depart and living Nature is spread out before my soul.
Goethe

Earthly limitations reduce spiritual thought to the words of human beings, yet in the depths of consciousness is preserved the imprint of the heavenly hieroglyphs.

The Teacher

No one is the creator of names but he alone who can perceive their true nature and can apply them in form, letters, and syllables.
Plato

The signs of the esoteric language are not arbitrarily devised but correspond to the forces at work in the world.

Rudolf Steiner

Words and thoughts produce geometric patterns in the astral light. Our feelings color these patterns revealing to the clairvoyant observer their quality. Chaotic thoughts create chaotic shapes. Dark thoughts, negative emotions and motives, produce dark muddy colors. The purer the thought the more beautiful will be the created images. Fundamental truths, when realized, produce those monumental thought-form which the Adepts of the Mysteries use, in a simplified form, as the alphabet of their sacred language. The script of this language of the gods arises from the simplified mirror images of forces at work upon the archetypal planes of existence. To gain an understanding of Sensa characters, therefore, it is first necessary to gain some knowledge of the fundamental principles upon which they are based. Master D.K. gives a few hints concerning the highest principles in the opening lines of *A Treatise on Cosmic Fire:*

> There is one Boundless Immutable Principle; one Absolute Reality that antecedes all manifested conditioned Being. It is beyond the range and reach of any human thought or expression. The manifested Universe is contained within this Absolute Reality and is a conditioned symbol of it. In the totality of this manifested Universe, three aspects are to be conceived.

The three primary aspects of the 'manifested Universe' can be described in terms of the divine Trinity (tri-unity) of all world religions—Father, Son, and Holy Spirit; Shiva, Vishnu, and Brahma, etc. These three aspects of the life experience are the essence, quality, and form nature of all things great and small.

Spirit	Soul	Body
Life	Consciousness	Form
Father	Child	Mother
Atma	Buddhi	Manas

Through the interaction of the Sacred Three arise the birth, growth and evolution of consciousness in all the kingdoms of nature.

The father unites with the mother to produce a child who grows into an adult. Shiva and Mother Parvati unite giving birth to the soul of the world, which evolves toward perfection. Spirit and matter unite to produce the spark of consciousness, which evolves into the Perfection of Wisdom. The Heavenly Father unites with the Holy Breath to produce a Son of God.

The Divine Mother, the third aspect of the Tri-unity represents the creative force behind the activity of the manifested universe. She is the universal ground, substance, and energy through which all manifestation makes its appearance, the divine theatre, the stage on which the great play of evolution is acted out. She is what science has been seeking form the beginning. She is the Cosmic Fire and the Radiant Light. She is the essential nature of the highest psychic energy (*Shakti*). She is the supreme vehicle for the manifestation of consciousness in form. She is the breath of life that vitalizes all living organisms. She is the WORD, as well as the descent of the WORD into the world as the Breath of Life.

The Son, the second aspect of the Tri-unity, is the Christos, the Buddha-Nature, the Soul, the seed of spirit eternally present within all beings. He is the root source of all sentiency, the consciousness principle, which grows, expands, and evolves into the highest primordial awareness, wisdom, and love.

The Father, the First Principle of the manifested Tri-unity of Life, is pure Being, Synthesis, Reality manifesting as the spiritual Will, the divine Impulse behind the evolution of consciousness and spirit.

Plato, in his *A Dialogue on Nature (Timaeus),* speaks of the three principles in this way:

> In all things we must make a threefold distinction and think of that which becomes [2], that in which it becomes [3], and the mold that it resembles [1]. We may indeed use the metaphor of birth and compare the receptacle to the mother, the model to the father, and what they produce between them to their offspring.

The great Bodhisattva Padmasambhava, who according to the Buddhist tradition renounced the highest nirvana in order to remained on Earth's sphere to aid in the evolution of the human consciousness, has said that the Perfection of Wisdom consists of four realizations in one:

1. Realization of the single origin,
2. Realization that arises as inspiration or blessing,
3. Realization of the secret meaning of the sacred letters,
4. And complete absorption into the fundamental nature of reality.[1]

Concerning the hidden meaning of the sacred letters he gives this hint: "The realization of the three sacred letters is a realization of the body, speech, and mind of the Buddha." In other words they represent the three divine principles as expressed through the three-fold nature of a perfected human being or Buddha. The 'three sacred letters' (AUM), as represents phonetically and symbolically the synthesis of the divine Three Principles, non-duality and duality, absolute and relative as a single unit.

Non-duality

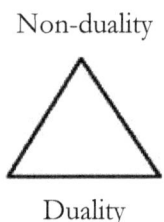

Duality

According to the *Pranavaveda*, an important esoteric scripture on the science of the Sacred Word, the secret meaning of the three letters (AUM) expresses the three highest principles of a human being, *Atma*, *Buddhi* and *Manas* (Pure Being, Primordial Awareness, and the Creative Mind).

---

[1] This quote is taken from *The Secret Garland of Vision*, which unlike most of the writings now attributed to Padmasambhava, was actually written and taught by him during his lifetime. The teaching is said to have been given to King Trisong Detsen by Padmasambhava before he left Tibet.

The Barddas, a collection of ancient Welsh manuscripts discovered in 1580, says that the original three sacred letters form the basis for all languages:

> From the three primary letters were constructed all the other letters. This is the primary secret of the Bards of the Isle of Britain. From this secret comes the knowledge of all alphabets.

Master D.K. divides the sacred WORD into SOUND, OM, and AUM. In this system the SOUND, also known as the Primordial Silence, corresponds to the first, or Spirit-*Atma* aspect of this vibrational tri-unity. The second aspect, depicted by the OM, symbolically represents the evolutionary keynote and impulse behind the ascent of the spirit along the Path of Return and its eventual perfection of wisdom. It corresponds to the second principle of *Buddhi*, spiritual awareness, wisdom and love. The third aspect, depicted by the AUM, symbolically represents the involutionary impulse behind the creativeness of spirit and the descent of the spirit into form. It corresponds to the third or Mother principle—M*anas*. "The entire story of incarnation," says D.K., "is hidden in the understanding of the SOUND and its differentiation into the OM and AUM."[1]

---

[1] *The Rays and the Initiations.* Page 201.

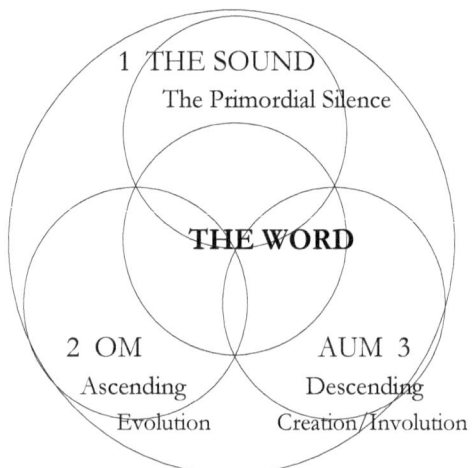

The AUM, when it is correctly sounded, causes the lunar builders (*Pitris*) to respond to the vibrations by creating those forms necessary for the descent of spirit into form. The OM, when correctly sounded, awakens the innate impulse within us to return to our original nature, the very essence of Being. But this 'sounding' should not be understood as an audible expression. A much higher creative process is implied, a process involving the mind and the higher feeling nature. When the scriptures instruct the yogi to sit quietly listening for the OM, it is not the ears that listen, but his whole being. Only when the yogi can sense, with her fine tuned feeling apparatus, the higher archetypal Vibration, can she begin to harmonize her own vibrations with it.

According to the *Pranava-Veda*, the Three Principles, active in all aspects of life, are embodied and symbolically expressed through the three letters of the sacred word—AUM.

The world is triple everywhere, in all its departments—Being [A], non-being [U], and their mutual pervasion, i.e., becoming

[M]. The three kinds of gunas or attributes, the three kinds of time,[1] three primary objects of enquiry; Prakriti or matter [U], Jivatma or soul [M], and Paramatma, the Supreme [A], birth, life, and death, etc. This trilateral tri-unity of the world is embodied in the three-lettered AUM. 'A' primarily stand for Atma, the Self; 'U' for anatma, the not-self; and 'M' for the Nishedha, the negation which is the relation, the bond between them.[2]

Like most true esoteric writing, this book is veiled in many respects. It nevertheless contains enough hints that through a careful reading a wealth of information may be obtained. The negation hinted at here pertains to the sense of separation of opposites that must be negated by the pilgrim (M) before liberation (*moksha*) from a false identification with the not-self (U) can be attained. It is the false-truth that is negated. To transcend the basic dualities of life the pilgrim must first clearly discriminate between them. Then he must negate the dominance of the lower polarities along with their separation tendencies, so that the realization of Essential Unity or Universal Synthesis occurs.

The activity of the three principles, represented by the AUM, can be understood from two perspectives. On the creative downward moving arc—A-father and U-mother join together to produce the M-child, which grows into an adult. On the evolutionary arch—the duality of A-father and U-mother is transcended by the M-primordial consciousness, or that which negates or dissolves the duality.

---

[1] Future, past, and present.
[2] *Pranava-Veda: The Science of the Sacred Word.* In 3 volumes. By Gargyayana, translated by Bhagavan Das, Theosophical Publishing, 1910.

When the 'A' and the 'U,' which represent the fundamental duality of life—spirit and matter, the infinite and the finite, non-relative and relative, reality and illusion, etc. are perceived as a unity they are, then according to the *sandhi* rules of Sanskrit grammar, the A sound is blended with the U sound to produce the O sound—the AUM thus becomes the OM.

In Sanskrit the 'M' sound is written as a single point. As the O sound, which represents the unity of spirit and matter, can be accurately depicted as a circle the OM can be depicted as a point within the circle.

Brother D.K., in volume five of his *A Treatise on the Seven Rays,* gives the following symbolic representation of the evolution of sacred Word:[1]

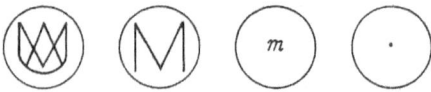

In the final image the O represents the inseparable synthesis (non-duality) of spirit and matter, while the point within it represents the inner spark of sentiency, the seed of spirit, the consciousness principle or soul.

---

[1] Page 55.

Of form and of consciousness the circle and the point are the natural symbols. This applies equally to an atom, a man, to a planet, and to a solar system.[1]

H.P. Blavatsky, in her *Theosophical Glossary*, defines the point within a circle in cosmic terms:

In its esoteric meaning the first unmanifested logos [the point] appearing on the infinite and shoreless expanse of Space, represented by the circle.

The Infinity of empty Space, the non-dual nature of spirit and matter, is represented by the circle. The Sanskrit numerical zero (*shunya*) is written as a circle. In Buddhist symbolism Emptiness (*shunyata*), [2] which like space is infinite, unbounded, and undifferentiated is often written as a circle.

In the metaphysics of India the circle-point represented the *Hiranyagarbha*, the living embryo/seed (*hiranya*) within the womb (*garbha*) of the Mother in union with the Father. In the human kingdom the point within the circle represents the *Tathagata-garbha*, the Buddha-Nature (*tathagata*) latent in all beings, within the universal ground of Being (*garbha*). According to Longchenpa primordial awareness is another name for the Buddha-nature. "Primordial awareness," said Padmasambhava, "is the heart of Emptiness."

---

[1] Alice Bailey, *Discipleship in the New Age, Vol II*, page 250
[2] The suffix 'ta,' in *shunyata* literally means 'the nature of,' in much the same way that the suffix 'ness,' as in emptiness.

To the Pythagoreans the point within the circle represented the monad, the One. In Greek philosophy, the monad applies not only to One Life but to any whole living system, great or small, that expresses a central spark of life through a united form.

In the Egyptian Mysteries, as well as in astrological symbolism, the point within the circle represents the hieroglyph of the sun, which was considered by Pythagoras and the ancient Mystery Schools to be a living organism. One of the fundamental ideas taught in these schools is the fact that the sun and the planets are the outer expressions, the vehicles, so to speak, of the great cellestial Gods. Master D.K. and Rudolf Steiner both confirm this. Our planet, when considered as a whole, can also be viewed as a single living organism, a vehicle for the planetary Logos. This is the basis of the 'Gaia hypothesis' that is being considered by some scientists. Goethe, who many consider as the father of the present day holistic movement, stated that Nature should be considered as a living, intelligent organism.[1] The Pythagoreans certainly believed this. Isaac Newton believed that the sun and planets were animate and not inanimate objects. He even theorized that gravity was the result of the attractive nature, the livingness, of celestial bodies. Unfortunately, all his scientific writings on the livingness of matter (hylozoism), were censored by the scientific community and never published.

According to Fabre d'Olivet, the author of *The Hebraic Tongue Restored*, the opening word of *Genesis*—Beraeshath, which is usually translated as 'in the beginning,' means beginning principle, from the Hebrew root ‫ראש‬ which means 'principle.' In hieroglyphic writing, he tells us, this first word was originally depicted thus ⊙.

---

[1] See Rudolf Steiner's *Introduction to the Scientific Writings of Goethe*.

The letter 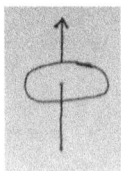 (the 'A' sound whose number is one) was depicted as a point, while the letter 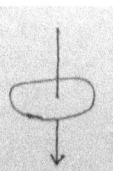 was expressed geometrically as a circle.

Numerically the circle is zero, while the point is one. This can be graphically represented by a veridical line (1), which depicts the upward growth or downward manifestation of the seed of spirit within the womb of the Mother.

The ancient Hermetic philosophers called the symbol of the circle-point, 'Sol,' from which we obtain the word solus, meaning sole or alone, and soul, the heart essence of any living organism, great or small.

According to Vajrayana Buddhism the three letters of the sacred word may be symbolically depicted thus:

In this image the seed of spirit or Buddha-nature, the spiritual essence hidden within all beings, is represented as rising up as a 'threefold spiraling vajra flame.' The crescent, which in the West is sometimes depicted as a chalice, represents the receptacle for the manifestation of the indwelling spirit.

The structure of the stupa, brilliantly illuminated for us by Adrian Snodgrass in his *The Symbolism of the Stupa*,[1] geometrically symbolizes

---

[1] Motilal Banarsidass, Delhi, 1992. This little known work is one of the greatest books available on sacred geometry.

the fundamental constitution of the evolution of consciousness. Note the symbolism of the threefold apex.

> It is the pathway of ascent, leading upward through the confining carapace of the physical world, passing beyond its limits and bounds to the unlimited and the unbounded. The axial pillar leads to the realm where the shackles of space and time are shaken loose. At the same time it forms a channel for the down flowing of reality into the less-then-real world, an influx that imbues the world with meaning, opening up the finite to the Infinite and time to the Eternal.[1]

From its imprisonment in matter, symbolized by the square, the 'womb four-square,' also called 'the lower four,' the seed of spirit ascends and is liberated in the supreme reality of its 'original state of being.' This idea is sometimes depicted symbolically by a pillar with a circle at the top ♀. Its number is 9. Its crown is initiation.

---

1 Page 163.

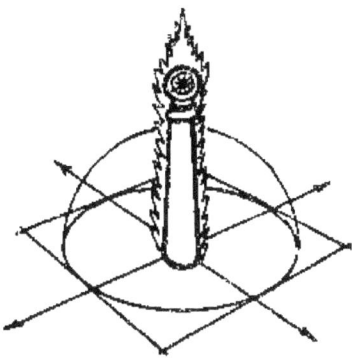

The Pythagoreans called it the 'Tower of Jupiter.' On an ancient coin Pythagoras is depicted as pointing to this tower.

The ancient Sages often depicted the spiritual principle of the central axis by the sign of the Tau (T) or Tao, which according to D.K. was the sacred word during the time of the ancient Atlantean civilization.[1] The Tau signifies the descent and 'Fulfillment of the WORD,' the birth, creation, and incarnation of spirit into form and latter the reverse, the ascent or Great Way leading to the 'End of the Great Work,' the death of the personality and resurrection of the Solar

---

[1] *A Treaties on White Magic*, page 478.

God in man. D. K. says that the Tau symbolizes 'reincarnation,' the continual birth, death and rebirth of the soul in form. In the Mithrian Mysteries during the festival of the resurrection of the sun each spring, the sign of the Tau (T) was written with ashes upon the forehead for those approaching initiation. This symbolic act depicted the descent of the WORD, as a divine Ray, upon the head of the initiate during initiation. The Tau glyph is used as the basis of many Sensa characters. It also forms a basis for the Sanskrit Devanagari, which according to Blavatsky was originally derived from Sensar.

संस्कृत शब्दकोष

Students of the Mystery Schools (*not to be found on the internet*) are taught that the WORD, as the creative vibrations of divine will and evolutionary creativeness, descend to this world from the spiritual Sun. Initiates of these schools learn to tap into this world power to further the 'Great Work.' The ritual use of this divine power was often symbolized by a mallet or gavel. In the hands of the Hierophant (Initiator) it symbolized his or her right to use this power as a representative of the Gods. This symbolic practice unconsciously continues to this day in boardrooms and courtrooms of America. It passed into public use by the Freemasons who had preserved its symbolic use without understanding much of its meaning, to the Sacred Mysteries.

The mallet [in Freemasonry] represents the sound of Nature, the Tao. It is not the name of God but rather of His Presence.[1]

In the Egyptian Mysteries the Ru or circle◯, symbolizes the Womb of Space, the origin and birthplace of the world. When

---

[1] Rudolf Steiner. *Freemasonry and Ritual Work*. Steiner Books, 2007.

combined with the creativeness of Nature, represented by the Tau (T), we have the Ankh, the sacred symbol for the birth, the creative manifestation, of life into form. It was used by the Egyptian Hierophants to invoke living spiritual energies from Ra the spiritual sun, as needed for the sake of the world. The Ankh is the symbol of life manifesting into form and giving livingness to the form. The Ankh represents the creative livingness descending (T) from the divine Source.

In the Egyptian Mysteries this 'word of power' was used to invoke the Light of Ra, the Spiritual Sun, during the death and rebirth of the spirit during initiation. The so-called Egyptian Book of the Dead is not, as many scholars believe, a manual for those approaching death; it is a guide for the candidates approaching initiation.[1] The Hierophant, the initiator, was often depicted as the holder of the Ankh.

In a similar way that the descending energy vibrations of the WORD are invoked during initiation, so the 'Great Invocation,' given to the public by Master D. K., is in one sense, a contemporary adaptation of the same process used by individuals and groups on a world scale to invoke the Spiritual Fire, and thereby hasten evolution, on three levels—the creative light or mind, love, and spiritual will. Devout Hindus practice a similar invocation where the energy (*shakti*) of the Savitri, the Goddess of the Sun, every morning at dawn, also three levels:

1) Prana, the vitality of the sun.
2) The energy of the 'heart of the sun,'
3) The highest energy from the Spiritual Sun.

---

[1] See *The House of the Hidden Places & The Book of the Master* by W. Marshal Adams.

This Gayatri mantra, which according to Hindu scriptures embodies the very essence of the Vedas, is said to be adapted from those true 'words of power' used by the Rishis to further and maintain the spiritual evolution of the world.

Maitreya, like the age of Aquarius which he represents, carries the ancient symbolism of the 'Water of Life,' a divine elixir of spiritual energy poured out as a fiery baptism (initiation) to all who will accept responsibility for its use. The Sensa glyph for Aquarius (≈) is also the Egyptian hieroglyph for 'rays of energy.'

The *Sepher ha Zohar (Book of Light)* symbolically describes the first act of creation as striking a spark from the Supernal Light and placing this spark in the center of a circle. From this point of light a fiery fountain is said to have spouted up. The material world, it states, is the result of the spiritual Light being reflected downward through this fountain. According to this teaching, *'Zohar,'* which means the radiant light of the central point (*nekuda reshima*), "the first manifestation of the Divine Unknown," manifests as the divine ray of creation.

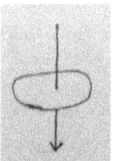

The divine ray manifests like all else in existence as a tri-unity of energies (*trikona* ⍭). To the 'Bards of the Isle of Britain,' these three energies were known as the 'Three Rays of the Sun,' the 'Three Pillars of Light,' and the 'Three Shouts spoken by God' during the creation of the world. In the secret script of their secret language, the Coelbren, these three primary Rays were depicted thus:[1]

---

[1] *Barddas* by Iolo Morganwg, Weiser Books 2002 (originally published 1862).

The Bards and Druids of ancient Britain called this symbol the 'Sacred Symbol of the unutterable name of God.' Gerald Massey, in his extensive study on the origin and evolution of language, *Natural Genesis,* (1883) states that this sign is the origin of the script of the letter A:

> The Chinese 'Three Lights' are likewise identical in origin and significance with the 'Three Shouts' of the British. The radical 'Ki' of 'Shi' is the sign of the Three Lights, according to Chinese etymologists, and this figure includes the *Triadic* form of the *biune one.*[1]

Note the Tau T glyph as the central pillar, ray, and path. The 'biune one' is the Divine Hermaphrodite. According to the *Barddas* the descent of the spiritual Light is represented by the letter I, which we are told, is really a substitute for the true sound, which is kept secret. This is consistent with the methods used by initiates where a blind is sometimes given to protect the Teaching from misuse. This kind of substitute, however, should not necessarily be considered false for it is often a correspondent in some way of the original and is therefore given as a hint. Egyptian Hieroglyphs depict the three primary rays of Ra, the hidden Sun, in a similar fashion:

---

[1] See volume 1 page 226.

The middle ray that streams from the Godhead, which the *Book of Light* calls the 'Central Pillar' (*tif'ert*), corresponds to the central magnetic axis of all life-forms, whether the magnetic axis of the human body, our planet, or the Solar System.

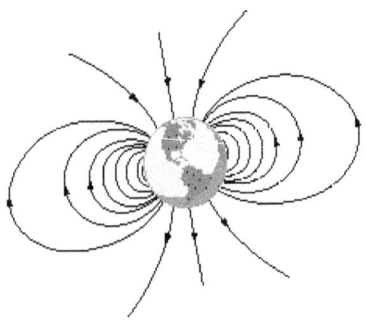

The Pythagoreans called the central axis of the Earth the 'Tower of Jupiter.' Proclus says that the 'Tower of Jupiter' represents the middle, summit, and center of the world and contains its generative power.[1] In the Vedic Mysteries the central axis of the Earth was called Mount Meru. Its correspondence in a human being is called the *sutratma*, the 'silver cord' that links the life of the body with the Higher Worlds.

---

[1] See his *Commentary on the Timaeus of Plato*, 2 volumes, Prometheus Press 1998.

The middle axis, along with the two currents, positive and negative, through which it streams, is represented in the Caduceus or the Rod of Hermes.

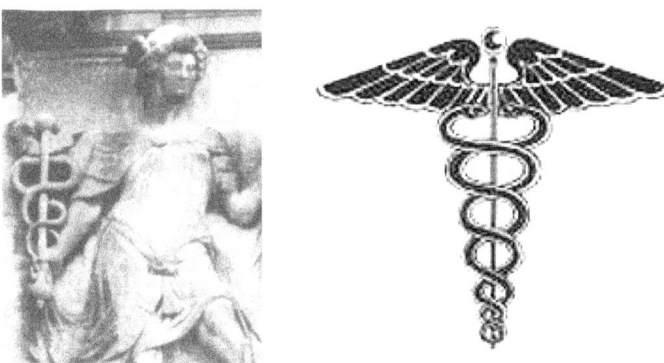

We must remember that geometrical Sensa symbols usually depict directional lines of force. When seen clairvoyantly the images often appear to be in motion.

---

[1] From an 18th century painting of the Kangra shool of India.

In the human kingdom the central pillar represents the Path itself, the antahkarana, the 'Middle Way' between the two extremes. It is the way of ascent uniting the consciousness of the seeker in meditation with the divine Presence.

The perception of spiritual reality involves the realization of the unity of the fundamental pairs of opposites—spirit and matter, non-relative and relative, unity and diversity, etc. To investigate relative truth or the matter extreme alone, as science is attempting to do, is to perceive only the outer shell, the effects, without understanding the essence, the causes of these effects. To investigate non-relative truth (the so-called absolute) alone, as the mystics are attempting to do, is to remove the ability to apply that truth in service to the world. To perceive and apply the whole truth, therefore, science and mysticism must come together. The balance point between these two extremes is the entrance to the Middle Way. This might be expressed geometrically thus:

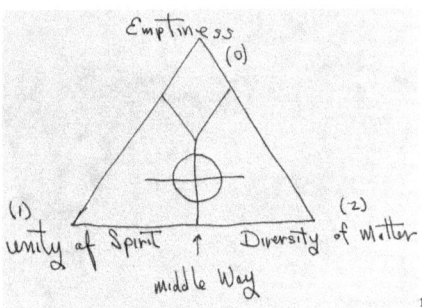

Unity of spirit and diversity of matter are opposites. Emptiness has no opposite.

When the sun and the moon currents are both fully energized and united in harmony the spirit enters the Path and ascends to unite

---

[1] This is also the solution to the formula puzzle given by D.K. on page 321 of his D.I.N.A. volume 2.

with the Infinite. In the body this corresponds to rising of the kundalini up the central channel behind the spinal column. The kundalini should never be forced. It arises naturally when the spirit unites with the Presence. The caduceus, therefore, represents the vital energies circulating through the etheric body on one level and the psychic energy of the yogi treading the Middle Path on another. That which takes place in the consciousness must also take place in the body; this is a basic law of nature. The Celtic Rose-Cross depicted below is similar in some ways to the caduceus. Note the double spiral of energies up the central axis.

The cross represents geometrically not only the ascent of the Spirit ↑ along its central axis but also the descent of Spirit ↓ into field of material nature.

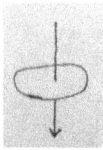 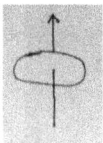

The cross was used by the Christians to demonstrate the descent and great sacrifice of the incarnation of Christ for the benefit of humanity. The upward ascent ↑ marks the middle path between the two extremes ✝ . As a fundamental principle the cross symbolizes the balanced union of Father Spirit (|) and Mother Nature (–), which produces the offspring (⊕), the Christos, the Buddha-nature, depicted in the Mysteries as the Rose and Cross ⊕.

*The vertical stream symbolizes the spirit-matter polarity. The horizontal axis signifies the male-female polarities of nature that must be unified and balanced before assent along the vertical axis can continue. The point of balance here is the fiery heart essence depicted geometrically at the center, at the point where the two lines of force cross.

Let us understand the heart as the focus of physical laws as well as the highest laws. This center was called the crossroad and was represented by an equilateral cross; the dorje, like the swastika, indicated the rotation of the fire of the heart....[1] Not without cause was the heart marked by the sign of the cross. Thus, the sign of the cross eternally accompanied the temple of the heart.[2]

---

[1] *Heart* 261
[2] *Heart* 4

The initiate consciousness is depicted symbolically as a rose and cross. The rose represents a point of fiery heart tension midway between the vertical path of ascent with the horizontal way of service to the world. In some teachings the four arms of the cross were said to correspond to the four directions.

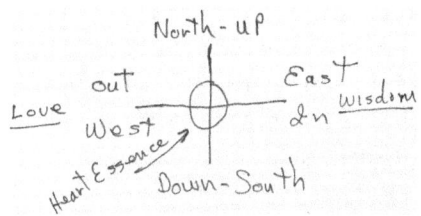

Love and wisdom are but two ways of expressing the same fiery magnet of the heart—outwardly as love and inwardly as wisdom.

At the top of our geometric paradigm we find the diamond mind, consisting of the Spiritual Triad $\triangle$—Atma, Buddha, and Manas—perfectly reflected in the soul of the Bodhisattva ∇ on the cross $\cdot\!\!\!+\!\!\!\cdot$.

According to Proclus the primary purpose of Pythagorean mathematics is to demonstrate the relationships that exist between the divine paradigms (spiritual archetypes) and their natural reflection in the world of form. Plato considered the synthesis, the resolution of the duality of opposites, particularly between the spiritual world and the world perceived by the senses, to be the very essence of mathematical philosophy.

Pythagorean mathematics can be applied in four fundamental categories:

1) Arithmetic — numbers at rest in space.

2) Geometry — the relationships between numbers at rest in space.

3) Music (harmony) — the harmonious relationships of numbers in motion through time.

4) Spherics (celestial harmonics) — the harmonious relationship between numbers in motion through time and space.[1]

Pythagorean Arithmetic and Geometry deal with numbers in space. Music and Spherics deal with numbers in time. Exoterically the science of spherics refers to astronomy, the cyclic (spiraling) motion of the heavenly bodies. Esoterically it pertains the natural correspondences that exist between the cyclic (spiraling) movement of celestial bodies through the heavens in correspondence to the cyclic (spiraling) evolution of consciousness. Pythagoras, as an initiate in the Egyptian and Orpheus Mysteries, undoubtedly understood these direct correspondences. The science of astrology should be understood in this way.

From the above we can begin to understand that the two-dimensional symbols used in the Mysteries are often but veiled simplified depictions of greater multidimensional models. They are geometric formulas that, from an intuitive perspective, point to rather than fully depict, a greater truth. It would be more accurate, for example, to depict a circle as a sphere and a square as a cube, etc. If we consider the symbol of a circle with a point at its center as representing a fundamental diagram of a living organism, or monad, evolving

---

[1] See part one of Proclus' commentary on Euclid's *Elements*. An excellent and very readable translation of this work was produced by Glenn R. Morrow in his: *Proclus: A Commentary on the First Book of Euclid's Elements*, Princeton University Press, 1970. Also see Thomas Stanley's *Pythagoras* a facsimile reprint of the chapter on Pythagoras from his *History of Philosophy* 1687, Philosophical Research Society, 1970 and Thomas Taylor's *The Theoretic Arithmetic of Pythagoreans*. Philosophical Research Society,

cyclically through time and space, then the circle can be viewed as but one whorl of a spiral, and the dot, the spark, seed-essence of that organism, becomes a line moving forward through the center of the spiral:

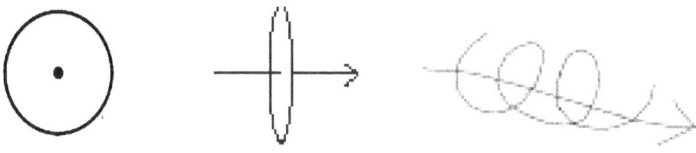

Plato, in his *Dialogues on Nature* (*Timaeus*) gives the following geometrical description of the activity or motion of a monad (organic whole).

> Of the seven kinds of motion given to the manifestation of the monad, that which is best suited to intelligence is the uniform circular motion around a single point. The Soul, which pervades the whole universe, was placed at the center. Around the Soul, at an equal distance, revolves the universe.

The term 'monad,' as used by the Pythagoreans, means the One, but it can also refer to any living *whole* system or organism. If we apply the Law of Analogy, 'as above so below,' we see that the orbital pattern of a body in motion around its essence or nucleus can be applied to planets revolving around the sun, or electrons around the nucleus of an atom or the personality around the soul. When viewed from the perspective of the evolution of consciousness, as represented in the geometric symbolism of the Stupa, the spiral becomes the cyclic progression of ascent around a vertical central axis:

H.P. Blavatsky, in her *Secret Doctrine*, writes,

The law of vertical movement in primordial matter is one of the oldest conceptions of Greek philosophy, whose first historical Sages were nearly all initiates of the Mysteries.[1]

This primary energy pattern, like the lines of force involved in all fundamental principles, can be analyzed according to the primary trinity of energies given above and will correspond to the three primary qualities or *gunas* of matter, inertia (*tamas*), activity (*rajas*), and rhythm (*sattva*), on one level and the three dimensions of a human being (*trikona* ♆): Psychic-energy (*shakti*), Sentiency (*nara*), and Will (*iccha*) on another.

Tamas/Shakti — 'rotary motion'

Rajas/Nara — 'spiral motion'

Sattva/Iccha — rhythmic 'forward progression' [2]

The ancient Egyptian *Hymns to Osiris* contains this interesting verse: "Oh Osiris, you revolve in the circle of Ra (the spiritual sun).... You are the great cyclist in the circle that moves forward as a mighty river."[3] This basic law of motion might be better understood if we compare it to the motion of all heavenly bodies spiraling through space, each around a greater center.

[1] Vol. 1, page 117.
[2] See *A Treatise on Cosmic Fire* By Alice A. Bailey p. 157-161
[3] p. 136

This illustration, from Edwin Babbitt's profound *Principles of Light and Color,* represents the fundamental cyclic activity of the energy of any whole system (monad), whether atomic, human or astronomical. To better understand, for example, how the subtle energy of the human etheric body circulates though the centers between its positive and negative polarities it might be useful to consult the third chapter of Babbitt's *Principles* (the original 560 page unabridged edition) on the etheric atom.

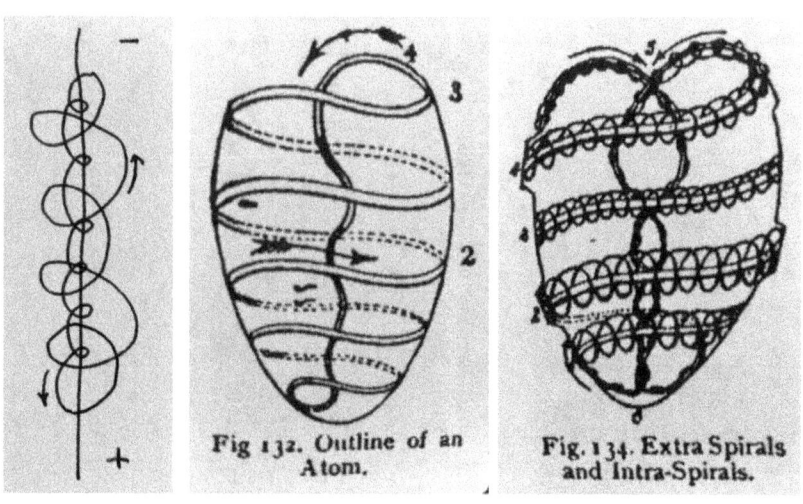

Fig 132. Outline of an Atom.

Fig. 134. Extra Spirals and Intra-Spirals.

As a primary symbol, the point within the circle ⊙, can be thought of as a cross-section, two-dimensional view, of a three-dimensional spiral in motion around a central axis, which is itself spiraling into a forth-dimensional forward progression around its greater center. This esoteric 'wheel turning upon itself' may have been what Plato was hinting at in his *Dialogue on Nature*:

> The Soul, which pervades the whole universe, was placed at the center. Around the Soul, at an equal distance, revolves the body of the world. This causes the circle itself to revolve in a circle.

Proclus, in his commentary on this verse writes:

> The divine Iamblichus correctly interprets the meaning of these words when he says that the circle is twofold, one being physical the other incorporeal, the former moving within the latter.[1]

In the East this idea is symbolized by the petals of a lotus; in the west by a rose or lily. The *Book of Light* states that "the beings created on the earth are symbolized as flowers."

The petals of the lotus, which Brother D.K. says symbolizes 'streams of whirling energy,'[2] can accurately depict the number of cyclic revolutions that any living organism, great or small, takes to spiral around its own inner nature, its 'jewel in the lotus.'

The Hindu Tantras symbolize the charkas (etheric nerve centers) as lotuses, the petals of which distinguish the quality of their energy. Each of these centers reflects an inner quality of consciousness expressed as active energies in the body. Accurate teaching on this

---

[1] *On Timaeus of Plato,* Book III.

[2] *A Treatise on Cosmic Fire* p. 833

subject can be found scattered throughout the Alice Bailey Books. As a flower opens its petals to the light of the sun so the centers open their petals to the light of the soul.

In the same way that the we speak of the greater Life 'in Whom we live move and have our being,' so the human body contains within itself many lesser life-forms, microorganisms, cells, nerve centers (*chakras*), etc., 'as above, so below.' This truth, that the greater includes the lesser, can be extended in kind to all life-forms great and small. The greater always includes the lesser. This is a fundamental doctrine of the Mysteries. The symbolism of the petals of the flower generally refers to the natural grouping of the united lives evolving around a greater life at their center, while each petal represents another lotus, another living organism, the petals of which each contains another lotus, ad infinitum.

As Rudolf Steiner once said: "There is only Being and beings, nothing else." In the final synthesis Being and beings are one and the same.

The third principle of the Tri-unity of life ♆, represented by the U sound of the AUM, governs the rhythmic ebb and flow of the creative activity of the mind, and by extension all natural and supernatural phenomena, from the cycles of day and night, the respiratory and circulatory system of the body, the greater cycles involving the spiritual evolution of consciousness (the descent into form and diversity and the returning ascent into greater unity) to the great in and out breath of Deity Itself. Abhinavagupta, in his *Paratrishika Vivarana*,[1] says that the two vibrations produced by the sound of the Sanskrit vowel U, long and short, represent expansion and contraction respectively. If we add to this what we know concerning their graphic and numerological equivalences these two primary complimentary and seemingly opposing forces they might be expressed as following:

U (Sanskrit) Expansion ℧ Evolution (9) ĺ In-breath, the Law of Attraction, centripetal force, subjective, gravitation.

ū (Sanskrit) Contraction Involution (6) ↓ Out-breath, the Law of Creation, centrifugal force, objective, radiation.

It might seem, at first glance, to be a contradiction to equate expansion and evolution with gravitation and centripetal force but we must remember that in the true evolutionary process we are concerned with an *inner* expansion, a magnetic gravitation toward an ever-greater more expansive essence of Being. Steiner and Blavatsky have both stated that in the physical world we live is a mirror image of reality and thus everything appears backwards and the reverse of its true nature. The spiritual Law of Attraction is reflected in the material world as the law of gravity but on 'a higher turn of the spiral' this law applies to the attraction of Spirit. It is no coincidence that the character we use to depict the number 6 is the symbol of involution, downward and outward, into form while 9 symbolizes the evolution, upward and inward, into spirit.

When the two directions, the creative out-breath and the evolutionary in-breath, are perceived as a single principle, as the ebb

---

[1] See Jaideva Singh's translation, *A Trident of Wisdom*, Motilal Banarsidass 1988

and flow, the cyclic pulsation, the rhythmic heartbeat, it is depicted graphically as a double spiral.

Vortex   Yin-Yang   Cancer

Adrian Snodgrass, in his brilliant work on the geometry of sacred architecture, *The Symbolism of the Stupa*, describes the symbol of the double spiral in terms of 'upward and downward flowing waters,' as seen, for example, in the cyclic activity of rain and evaporation.

> At the most universal level of meaning the upward and downward flowing waters represent the interaction of forces or currents emanating from the complementary poles of manifestation, namely *purusa* and *prakriti*, Heaven and Earth, Essence and Substance. This is the significance of the double spiral, found, for example, at the ends of the rainbow shaped torana-lintels at Sance. The two spirals represent the forces emanating from the two poles of the World Egg, one rolling upward and the other downwards, produced by the Egg's rotation around the axis that joins the two poles.[1]

---

[1] Page 296-297

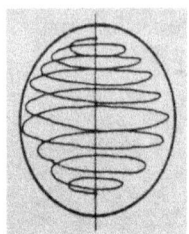

This idea is also expressed in the yin-yang symbol of Chinese Taoism. One of the earliest known appearances of this symbol can be traced to Zhang Huang's *Compendium of Diagrams*.[1]

Walter Russell in his somewhat overlooked masterwork, *The Secret of Light* uses the double spiral as a spatial model for the duality of energy—gravitation and radiation, which is the expression of the duality of the laws of attraction and repulsion:

---

[1] University of Chicago Library, East Asian Collection.

The Mystery Of

Gravitation & Radiation

This principle is expressed as the involution (creation) and evolution (assension) of the One.

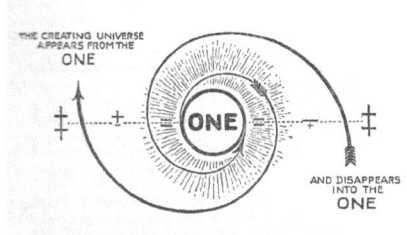

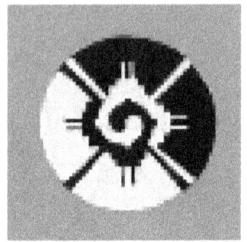

Indian   Mayan

The double spiral also makes its appearance in the astrological sign of Cancer ♋ (♋-69), which in one sense signifies the gateway between death and rebirth.[1] In a lecture by Rudolf Steiner given March 14, 1907 he discusses the symbolism of the double spiral from the perspective of the Rosicrucians:

> A widely used esoteric sign is the so-called vortex. It can be thought of as two intertwined number sixes. This sign is used to indicate and characterize a certain type of event that can occur both physically and spiritually. For example, a developing plant will finally produce seed from which new plants similar to the old one can develop. To think that anything material passes from the old plant to the new is an unfounded materialistic bias and will eventually be proved wrong. What passes to the new plant are formative [etheric] forces. As far as matter is concerned, the old plant dies completely; materially its offspring is a completely new creation. This dying and new becoming of the plant is indicated by drawing two intertwining spirals—a vortex, which is drawn so that the two spirals do not touch ☺. Many events, both physical and spiritual, correspond to such a vortex. For example, spiritual research shows us that the transition from the ancient Atlantean culture to the first post-Atlantean culture can be represented by such a vortex.... The spiritual aspect of that ancient culture vanished and a new culture arose. The esoteric

[1] See *Esoteric Astrology* by Alice Bailey p. 33

sign of the vortex depicts that event. The inward spiral indicates the old civilization and outward-turning spiral the new. During the transition from the old culture to the new, the sun rose in spring in the constellation of Cancer...[6520 BC] [1] The transition from Atlantis to post-Atlantis took place under the constellation of Cancer, whose sign is the intertwining spirals [♋].[2]

In another lecture Steiner continues with this idea from another perspective:

When the human being sinks into sleep, his astral body and ego... withdraw from the physical and etheric bodies. When you observe a sleeping human being clairvoyantly, the physical body and the etheric body lie there in the bed. These two members remain connected whereas the astral body emerges together with the higher members. With clairvoyance we can see how, when sleep begins, the astral body, bathed in a kind of light, draws out of the other two bodies. To describe this condition with greater exactitude we must say that the astral body of modern man appears as if it consisted in many streams and sparkles of light and the whole appears like *two intertwining spirals,* as if there were two figure-sixes, one of which vanishes into the physical body, while the other extends far out into the cosmos like a trail of a comet. Both of these trails of the astral body very soon become invisible in their further extensions, so that the phenomenon then has an ovoid shape. When the human being wakes the trail no longer extends into the cosmos and everything draws again into the etheric and physical bodies.[3]

---

[1] This date for the beginning of the 5ᵗʰ Race (Atlantis being the 4ᵗʰ) is in accordance with the Teachings of Rudolf Steiner, who divides the sub-races according to the progression of the spring equinox through Zodiacal signs.

[2] See *The Secret Stream: Christian Rosenkreutz and Rosicrucianism,* edited by Christopher Bamford.

[3] From a course of lectures given in Munich May 1907, also found in *Theosophy of the Rosicrucian,* 1981, p. 30.

This principle is active within the etheric body as the coordinated interaction between the upward moving subtle energies (*prana*) and the downward moving subtle energies (*apana*) producing the cyclic activity of the breath, the circulatory system, the nerve impulses, as well as the circulation of the subtle energies of the *chakras*. According to the *Kalachakratantra*, "yoga is the union of *prana* and *apana*." The unity and equilibrium of these two seemingly opposing, yet complementary currents through the unifying activity of the heart.[1] Titus Burckhardt in his illuminating treatise, *Alchemy: Science of the Cosmos, Science of the Soul*, states:

> The sun's course, in so far as it appears above the horizon, follows an increasingly wide circle from the winter solstice to the summer solstice, and then an increasingly narrow circle until the full year comes round. Basically this corresponds to an 'unwinding', spiral which, after so many turns, becomes a 'winding-up', spiral – an image which has been portrayed in a variety of signs, such as the double spiral, the twofold spiral vortex, familiar as the Chinese *yin-yang*, and not least in the staff of Hermes *(caduceus)* in which two snakes are entwined on an axis –the world axis. The opposition made in the sun's course (the ascending and the descending) corresponds in a certain sense to the opposition between heaven and earth—with this difference, that here both sides are mobile, so that, instead of an opposition of causes, it is a question of an alternation of forces.[2]

The union of these two forces from a vertical perspective can be expressed geometrically as a six-pointed star . This symbol demonstrates the unity and interconnectedness of the macrocosm and microcosm, heaven and earth, higher and lower mind, spirit and matter, etc. It also demonstrates the merging of the

---

[1] See Rudolf Steiner's *Spiritual Science and Medicine* Lecture # 2 concerning the activity of the heart in the balancing the upper and lower energies of the body.

[2] p. 44

involution/creation ∇ currents with evolution/ascension Δ currents. Another way in which the union of the two forces, higher and lower, are sometimes depicted geometrically is through the glyph $\oplus$.

Only a few examples can be given to the public concerning the hidden meaning of esoteric symbols. H. P. B., in one of her private papers to the Esoteric Section of the Theosophical Society, gives the following diagram to show the relationship of the Three Principles.

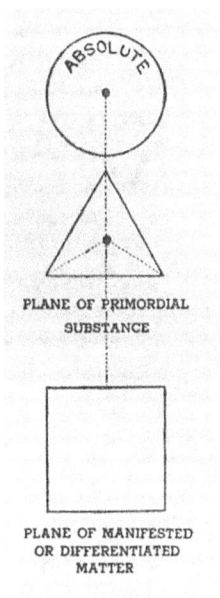

PLANE OF PRIMORDIAL
SUBSTANCE

PLANE OF MANIFESTED
OR DIFFERENTIATED
MATTER

In another diagram by her, from the January 1900 issue of the Theosophist, she demonstrates the Three Principles through three fundamental symbols. They have specific meaning in relation to the area of their application, which is often expressed by the symbol that they are included within.

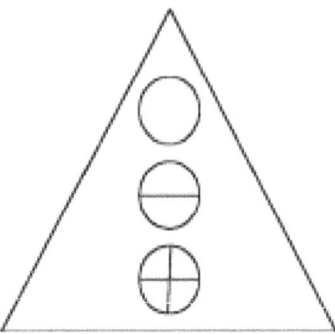

Rudolf Steiner also depicts the Three Principles thus:

1   2   3

The mysterious pentagram ☆ pertains to Manas, the third principle, the creative mind. In relation to the evolution of a human being it demonstrates pictorially the unification through self-mastery of the 'five planes of the human evolution' reached by an Adept— 3) higher mind, 4) the four-fold personality, 5) the lower mind, 6) the emotional nature, and 7) the physical/etheric body. 4 through 7 are but reflections of the third principle manas or mind, and therefore have no life of their own.

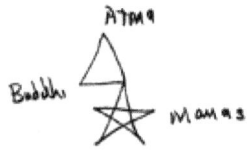

H.P. Blavatsky graphically expresses this idea in her Instructions to the Esoteric Section thus:

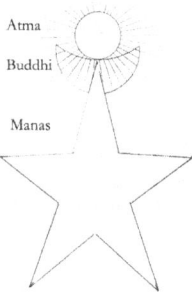

The great evolutionary cycle ☽, the descent of spirit into the form and back again to essential unity, can be depicted through a definite sequence of symbols. Master D.K., in his *Letters on Occult Meditations*, gives the following hint:

> The Master is one who has blended all the lines of fivefold development first into the three and then into one. The six-pointed star becomes the five-pointed star, the cube becomes the triangle, and the triangle becomes the one; whilst the one (at the end of the greater cycle) becomes the point in the circle of manifestation.

Each stage of the evolution of consciousness (initiation) is marked by a geometric sign. More on this can be found in the occult classics, *A Treatise on Cosmic Fire*, *The Key to the Universe*, *The Key to Destiny*, and the *Symbolism of the Stupa*.

A Sensa symbol can be arranged in several ways all of which must to be understood and mastered by the disciple—theoretically, visually, and in practical application. "Each of these words will convey a specific meaning and when rightly understood will bring about changes in the disciple's life, in his service and therefore in his effect within the Ashram."[1]

---

[1] Discipleship in the New Age, Vol. 2 (page 133).

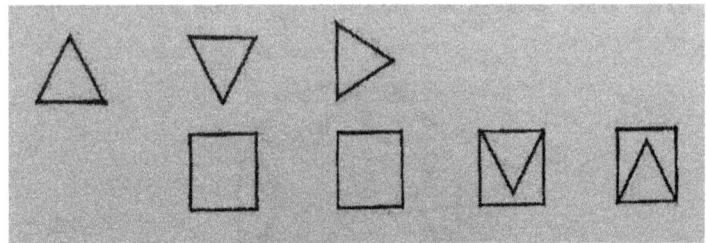

The relationship between aspects of a geometric symbol, the dominance of one aspect over another, as well as the direction of its lines of force, are determined by its positioning. In all cases the symbol will demonstrate the movement and relationship of *energies*, physical, etheric, mental or spiritual, as well as the kind, quality, direction, and dominance of those energies. An upper aspect of the image will usually represent a dominating influence over a lower. For example, the glyphs of Venus and Terra ♀ ♁, express the fact that their dominating energies of spirit ◯ and form + reversed. 'Up and down' symbolize greater and lesser, spirit and matter, etc. 'Right and left' refer to positive and negative polarities respectively on the horizontal or level plane. 'Internal and external' means just that.

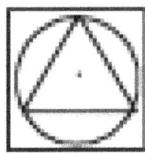

The above arrangement depicts an average human being, with the central seed of spirit, 'the jewel in the lotus,' a threefold inner nature or soul △, which is hidden, separated in consciousness, from a fourfold outer nature or maya □, which imprisons it in form. Students of the Rosicrucians have often used his symbol without explanation meaning a human being. The circle, which has multiple levels of corresponding meaning, can represent what initiates called the 'ring pass not' or 'auric egg.' In this symbol the influence of the inner spiritual nature has not yet extended to the outer form, the four-fold personality on the physical plane. By adding petals and or other signs we can make our symbol-signature more specific.

Paracelsus gives some interesting hints on this question in his *Aurora of the Philosophers:*

> Magic, it is true, had its origin in the divine ternary, the Tri-unity of God. For God marked all his creatures with this ternary and engraved its hieroglyph on them with his own finger. Nothing in the nature of things is or can be produced that lacks the magistery of divine ternary (3). In it is contained the all the secrets of nature and the four elements, for the Ternary (3) plus the magical Quaternary (4) produces a perfect Septenary (7), which is endowed with many arcana. It arises from the Light of the World on the horizon of eternity and by the assistance of God it gives us the complete bond of unity. It also refers to the virtues and operations of all creatures and to their use, since they are all stamped and marked with their arcana, signs, characters and figures so that there is left in them scarcely the smallest occult point which is not made clear on the examination. When the Quaternary and Ternary mount to the Denary (10) then is accomplished their reduction to unity

The three and four become seven and when united with the primordial Tri-unity, becomes the perfect ten, which is One, the Monad, but at a higher octave. $3 + 4 = 7 + 3 = 10 = 1$

Georg Von Welling, a German student of the Rosicrucians, in 1719 wrote a remarkable esoteric work entitled *Opus Mago-Cabbalisticum et Theosophicum (The Great Magical Theosophical Cabbal),* which was intended only for "intimate conversations." But "because the first volume of this work was made public against our will, we thought it wise to add the second and third volumes for the sake of completeness." Joseph G. McVeigh has accomplished a good translation into English from this massive and very esoteric German work. Weiser Books published it in 2006. While the alchemical aspects of the text are veiled in the usual Hermetic symbols there are enough clues and hints and even outright plain speaking to make many aspects of this lost science reasonably understandable. It is basically an esoteric treatise on the Three Principles, which according the usual alchemical correspondences he calls—mercury, sulfur, and salt. He reveals the significance of many geometric symbols. Manly P. Hall, in his *Secret Teachings of All Ages,* devoted a chapter to these symbols, which he called, *Fifteen Rosicrucian and Qabbalistic Diagrams.* This work is a rich source for understanding the esoteric script. Von Welling gives the signs for the elements on two levels, the crude elements and the invisible etheric elements, which, he says, were of Eden, the etheric plane, before the fall.

	Air	Fire	Water	Earth
Crude elements	△	△	▽	▽
Invisible [Etheric Elements	△	△	▽	▽

The seeming error of listing eight instead of seven might be reconciled when we consider that the element fire, like its higher counterpart manas or mind, is often divided into higher and lower, in this case invisible and visible fire.

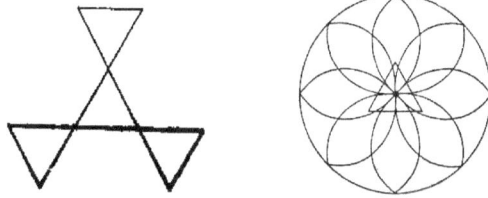

To understand the Three Principles, the Tri-unity, in relation to the evolution of consciousness we must be able to apply it on both the involutionary downward arc of creation and the evolutionary upward arc of the Path. When the creative downward arc is being considered the three principles will correspond to Father and Mother uniting to produce a Child.

Father   Mother

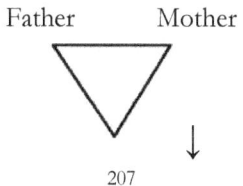

Child

On the evolutionary arc this process is reversed and the divine Child, the 'prodigal son,' returns home to collect his inheritance by uniting the pairs of opposites, positive and negative, and then by following the Middle Path, as taught by the Buddha, between them and eventually transcending them in such a way as to include them as well.

Emptiness (non-dual)

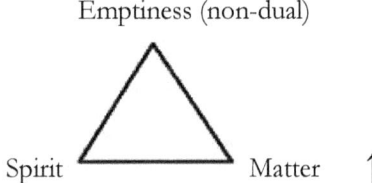

Spirit   Matter   ↑

The Sensa alphabet can be expressed numerically, geometrically and harmonically. To do this accurately the Scribes of Hermes must first work the correspondences that naturally exist between number, color, sound and the geometric patterns that depict their motion, their lines of force. He must correlate this understanding with the numerical and geometrical sequence of the creative process of descent ▽ (1-3-7-12) on one hand, and the evolutionary process of ascent △ (12-7-3-1) on another. The esoteric script of the language of the Gods thus accurately expresses both the process of Creation, the implementation of the Divine Plan and the Path of Return to the Source and Essence of our Being.

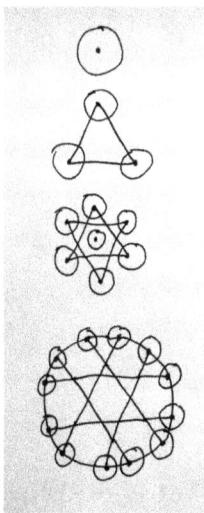

Many more examples could be given but this will suffice for the time being. I leave it to my intuitive brothers and sisters to take it to its next level of usefulness.

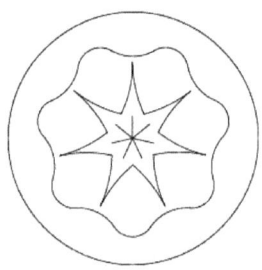

Signatures of Living Organisms

Nature has given signs to everything whereby they are known. This is the Language of Nature, which signifies for what everything is good for. In this lies the mystery and central science of the highest philosophical works and the true healing arts.   Jacob Boehme

All creatures are stamped and marked with their particular occult signs, characters, and figures, so that even their smallest aspects are revealed when these signs are examined.
Paracelsus

Thus amidst the raging fire one can see a thin sword above the forehead of the warrior of spirit.   .
Heart

One of the ways by which a Master can evaluate the student's progress, inner qualities and abilities is by observing the archetypal signatures displayed in fiery symbols above his head.

As an open book the personality of a man is inscribed above his head as the constantly flaming signature of his essence. One may read it even with plain observation.[1]

This level of spiritual clairvoyance seems to be somewhat rare though a number of seers have written about it.[2] Nancy Lansdale had this type of mental clairvoyance. She investigated this curious phenomenon with the idea of later writing a book on the subject. Unfortunately it was never finished due to her untimely passing. Theodore Heline, partner of the well known esoteric writer Corinne Heline, obtained portions of Lansdale's unfinished work and wrote a short pamphlet on it entitled *The Archetype Unveiled*. This fascinating work includes a few tantalizing reproductions of her drawings along with an analysis of some of the symbols.[3]

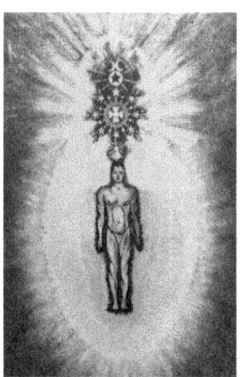

According to Nancy Lansdale every living organism has its own graphic signature, which manifests as a set of symbols that in a

[1] Agni Yoga 330

[2] The Agni Yoga Teacher, Master D. K., Rudolf Steiner, Paracelsus, Jacob Boehme, Uniche, H. P. Blavatsky and Nancy Lansdale to name the few that I know of.

[3] *Archetype Unveiled: A Study of the Sound Patterns Formed by the Creative Word.* by Theodore Heline, *New Age Press* 1965. Theodore and Corinne Heline were students of Max Heindel and Alice Bailey.

pictorial sense represents its true name. It reveals, for those with eyes to see, the organism's fundamental characteristics, its rank on the evolutionary ladder of life, its primary and secondary purpose, and the keynotes of its essential nature. From the observations made by Nancy Lansdale these signatures change very slowly, if at all, during a single life-time of the organism. The signatures of trees and plants appear below the roots in a yellow light. She also recorded in drawings the signatures of many famous people.

Sir Winston Churchill   Chiang Kai-Shek

Blavatsky, in one of the notes to her esoteric classic, *The Voice of Silence*, which she translated from the original Sensar (Sensa), says that each stage of Raja Yoga is secretly depicted by a geometric symbol that blazes above the head of a yogi. She does not give these symbols for as she says of one of them, "it is sure to be pounced upon by some charlatans and desecrated in its use for fraudulent purposes." But she does give this hint:

> The star that burns overhead is the 'star of initiation.' The caste-mark of Saivas, devoties of the sect of Siva, the great patron of all yogins, is a black [indigo] round spot, the symbol of the sun now perhaps, but that of the star of initiation in Occultism in days of old.

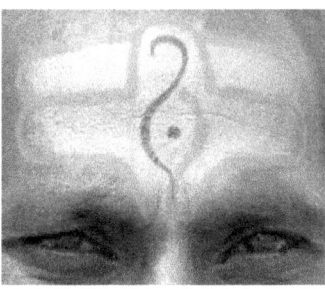

Brother D.K., in a letter to one of his disciples, gave the following instructions.

> Attempt, as a soul, to link up with your co-disciples. Having done this, seek to see the symbol which blazes forth from the brow of each of them. Each symbol is different. Endeavour to see these symbols by definitely linking up with and pouring out love to your brothers. Note down each day the symbol that seems to you to be related to them.[1]

D.K. is generally silent on the subject of signatures although here and there he gives a few more hints:

> Each life that the Personality leads is, at the close, represented by some geometrical figure, some utilization of the lines of the cube, and their demonstration in a form of some kind. Intricate and uncertain in outline and crude in design are the forms of the

---

[1] *Discipleship in the New Age* Volume 1, page 308-309

earlier lives; definite and clear in outline are the forms built by the average advanced man of this generation. But when he steps upon the Path of Discipleship, the purpose consists in merging all these many lines into one line, and gradually this consummation is achieved. The Master is He Who has blended all the lines of fivefold development first into the three, and then into the one. The six-pointed star becomes the five-pointed star, the cube becomes the triangle, and the triangle becomes the one; whilst the one (at the end of the greater cycle) becomes the point in the circle of manifestation.[1]

Look for those who have blended head and heart and above whose foreheads shines the mystic symbol of the builder.[2]

Seek for the symbol to be found above the head of each of your co-disciples. This is an interesting form of work and for you at this time most developing.[3]

The five-pointed star at the time of initiation on the mental plane flashes out above the head of the initiate.[4]

From clairvoyant seers such as Lansdale and others we learn that all life-forms great or small have their own symbol signatures. Paracelsus used this information to perform the many remarkable cures that other physicians named incurable. By observing the esoteric signature of plants, he tells us, one may intuitively understand their healing purpose. The science of signatures can also be applied to those composite or group lives we call families, clans, races, countries and Ashrams. When applied to families and clans they fall into the domain of Heraldry, the origin of which can be esoterically traced to the sacred Mysteries. In ancient times the 'Herald,' was an initiate who acted as an intermediary between the inner Temple and the kings, noblemen and major families of the time. He gave to them certain symbols

---

[1] *Letters on Occult Meditation*, page 5.

[2] *DINA* Vol 1 page 145

[3] *Desipleship in the New Age*. Vol 1 page 267

[4] A Treatise on Cosmic Fire page 696

appropriate for their use. The pure geometry of their hidden names however was often veiled behind corresponding natural forms, such as those of animal or other objects.

When applied to countries these esoteric signatures were once classified under the ancient name of Hestery. Unich, in her mysterious and insightful *Mysteries of Isis* (1858) says that the ancient term Hesta was used to represent those symbols which outwardly depict their inner archetypal or spiritual nature of a nation. A country's flag or seal will often contain a symbolic depiction of its true geometric signature just as the coat-of-arms often contains a portion of the true signatures of a powerful family or clan. Unich writes:

> [These symbols] represent the presence and support of those unseen spiritual powers who preside over the nation or government…. Every nation, therefore, had its tutelary and protecting gods and goddesses to whom it paid the highest honor and devotion and its particular Hesta, distinguishing it from other nations…. But as the Hesta of any nation is attributed to the Fates the interpretation of its symbols may justly be suspected to give the spiritual origin of its race and the prominent characteristics, *which afford the correct presage of their future and ultimate destiny*…. This origin, together with our [USA] future destiny, like that of other nations, may be suspected to be found in the symbols of our Hesta.

The 'all seeing eye' in the triangle above is a symbol that was used in the Sacred Mysteries and is still used in Freemasonry. It depicts the Spiritual Triad of the Divine Presence within us.

From this it should not be too difficult to perceive the latent possibility of a new science. Through an examination of the these energy-signatures the seers of the future will be able to very accurately diagnosis physical, psychological, and spiritual difficulties, determine one's station on the Path, and even provide a visual representation of the student's archetypal potential. Due to the great hastening of evolution that is now taking place new applications of psychic energy for the common good become a real possibility. This work, though incomplete, is written with the intention of providing a framework for this new field of exploration. And while it is sure to contain errors, it nevertheless warrants further investigation. It is my ardent wish that a few open-minded scientists and physicians will seek the practical applications of psychic-energy for the benefit of the world and the elimination of suffering.

∴

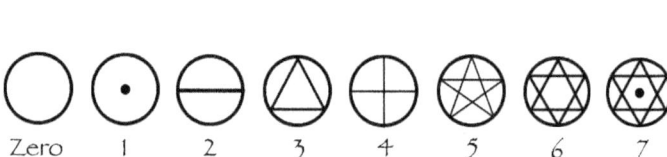

3 Divine Principles
7 Planetary Gods
12 Zodiacal Gates

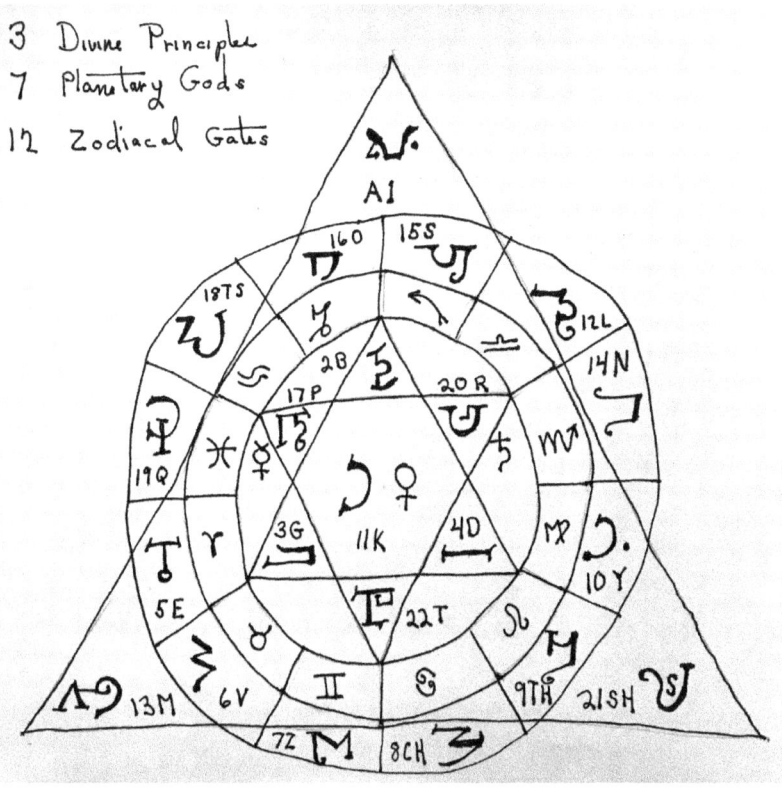